Shaping a Faithful Life

Shaping a Faithful Life
Discernment and Discipleship for Young Adults

Kathleen Henderson Staudt

 Morehouse Publishing
NEW YORK

Unless otherwise noted, the scripture quotations contained herein are from the New Revised Standard Version Bible, copyright © 1989 by the Division of Christian Education of the National Council of Churches of Christ in the U.S.A. Used by permission. All rights reserved.

Church Publishing Incorporated
19 East 34th Street
New York, NY 10016

Cover design by Jennifer Kopec, 2Pug Design
Typeset by Progressive Publishing Services

A record of this book is available from the Library of Congress

ISBN-13: 978-1-64065-443-3 (pbk.)

For David and Sarah
In shared adulthood

Contents

Contents

Acknowledgments and Permissions

This project has emerged over many years, beginning with a grant from the Episcopal Evangelical Education Society that enabled me to test and develop these materials with a number of different young adult groups. I am grateful to all the young adults who have shared their stories and tried out these practices with me over the years: the Progressive Christian Young Adults groups at Vienna Baptist Church; the campus communities of Brent House at the University of Chicago; the Canterbury Club at Michigan State, and the University of Maryland College Park; the clergy friends who supported me in this work, especially Stacy Alan, Kit Carlson, Peter Antoci, and Jenifer Gamber; and the Center for Lifetime Learning at Virginia Theological Seminary, led by Diane Wright and Lisa Kimball, where I have had regular opportunities to invite people into these practices. We learn so much from one another's stories and this whole project has been a rich collaboration.

I am grateful to Graywolf Press for permission to quote from William Stafford, "The Way It Is" from Ask Me: 100 Essential Poems. Copyright © 1977, 2004 by William Stafford and the Estate of William Stafford. Reprinted with the permission of The Permissions Company, LLC on behalf of Graywolf Press, Minneapolis, Minnesota, graywolfpress.org.

Grateful acknowledgement is also made for permission to quote from *Wishful Thinking* by Frederick Buechner. Revised and Expanded. Copyright © 1973, 1993 by Frederick Buechner. Used by permission of HarperCollins Publishers.

My own poems are reprinted with permission as follows:

Kathleen Henderson Staudt, "What I Remember," in *Waving Back: Poems of Mothering Life* (Georgetown, KY: Finishing Line Press, 2009).

Kathleen Henderson Staudt, "In the Cool of the Evening," in *Annunciations: Poems Out of Scripture* (Eugene, OR: Wipf and Stock, 2018).

Kathleen Henderson Staudt, "Reveling," in *Good Places: Poems* (Georgetown, KY: Finishing Line Press, 2017).

Kathleen Henderson Staudt, "Unknowing," in *Good Places: Poems* (Georgetown, KY: Finishing Line Press, 2017).

Kathleen Henderson Staudt, "Stumbling Credo" (unpublished poem, 2019).

Introduction

If you are in your twenties or thirties—whether a student, entering the workforce, on your own for the first time, or perhaps living with family while trying to figure out "what's next"—chances are that you are vividly aware of life questions about meaning, purpose, and identity. When these questions loom large, it helps to find and connect with others at the same stage of life who are asking similar questions.

Down through the ages, our Christian tradition has invited people to approach these questions by "discernment"—the spiritual practice of attending to God's presence and desire in the choices life presents to us. This workbook is designed to engage you in various approaches to discernment as you seek to explore the deep questions of meaning and purpose that have always been at the heart of the Christian journey. You can use it on your own or, perhaps better, as the core of a conversation with others at a similar stage of life and on the same journey. Along the way, we will see how the practice of discernment nourishes and informs the call to faithful living that the tradition has called "discipleship."

Young Adults and "Church"

As you seek companions in this process of discernment, you may find that people in their twenties and thirties who are drawn to a church-identified community often have little in common aside from the fact that they all are in this group. Their lives may or may not intersect in any other way. Some may be married, some single; their professions, interests, and temperaments may be quite different. Yet for some reason, they are all being drawn to something that the church may have to offer.

xii | Shaping a Faithful Life

This series of workshops invites young adults to pay attention to the deep questions they are asking as they seek to shape a faithful life, and to see where their particular experiences meet the call to transformation that is at the heart of Christian faith.

We know that adults tend to learn the tradition not so much by receiving instruction as by sharing with one another the parts of it that make sense of their lives, and by working with mentors who can talk freely about ways that scripture, liturgy, and the life of prayer are alive and meaningful in their lives. Accordingly, this set of resources invites a series of questions that can lead to conversation about the resources that Christian faith offers for shaping a faithful life. I have tested these both with campus ministry groups and with parish-based young adult groups. In both contexts, participants have found that the process of focusing on questions, rather than answers, is an effective way to enter a deepening practice of discernment in community, and to open up new visions of what a faithful and meaningful life looks like.

Discernment and Discipleship: Defining the Words

Discernment and *discipleship* may not be terms that are familiar to everyone, so let's start with some definitions. *Discernment* comes from a Latin root that point to a process of sorting out, distinguishing among options. *Discernment* is the practice of attending to God's presence and seeking direction, not only at times of urgent decision making but, indeed, at all times in our lives. Discernment involves asking questions whose answers we're not sure about. We may even be so afraid of the answers that we hesitate to ask the questions: Should I choose this path rather than that one? What is the meaning of the experience I am having? What is the most faithful choice in this situation? Christian traditions of discernment almost always involve conversations with others who are on the same journey. The Ignatian tradition does this in consultation with a spiritual guide or director; Benedictine discernment is practiced in the context of community life and meditation on scripture; Quakers seek clarity through prayerful listening and consultation with a "clearness committee" (the model for what I will call a "clarity team"). *Shaping a Faithful Life* adapts methods from these and other approaches to discernment in order to help you see what rich resources Christian spiritual practice offers for the questions most central to your life.

Discipleship: The Shape of a Faithful Life

An important outcome of faithful discernment is greater commitment to discipleship — to a way of life informed by practices that help us to "follow Jesus" as we come to know his presence in our lives. This is the journey of every Christian, of course: to discern how I, in particular, am called to live out my faith. In early adulthood, it's important to explore our language about discipleship and to ask questions: What does it mean to follow Jesus in our time? What doesn't it mean? Because these are important questions at every stage of the life of faith, each session of this program includes invitations to study scripture, especially the stories and teachings of Jesus, to help you articulate and ask more deeply what difference it makes to choose the biblical story, especially the Jesus story, as the story that can make sense of your life experience. Using these resources, the program invites you to ask: What is the work that God is doing in the broken world of today? And what is my piece of that work?

Meaning-Making in the Now: Identity and Community

Sociologist Sharon Daloz[1] reminds us that, for younger adults especially, faith is not always about "belief" but is rather a process of "meaning-making." The journey of faith is a journey toward making sense of our world, beginning where we are. As you enter and claim adulthood, it is important to find safe places to sort out your own ways of making sense of the world. You may need to ask honestly, for example: How is my lived experience different from traditions I've inherited from my family, and from the many voices in the surrounding culture that seek to define me? What can I really claim as my own particular identity, in a culture where I am labeled in all kinds of ways — as a member of a generation (Gen X, Gen Y, Millennials, Gen Z) — as a cohort of consumers? These understandings of common values of a cohort may seem to be important steps in the journey of identity formation and of faith, but most people as they enter adulthood also need, and seem to crave, invitations to ask deeper and more fundamental questions like: Who am I now? What is it about me that I can claim apart from the expectations of others? What and whom do I love? Where is my passion? And how does all this connect to my deepest values, to my life of faith?

Parks[2] points out that for many young adults there are two great yearnings working together: the desire to claim individual agency or xiv | Shaping a Faithful Life

identity, and the desire to belong to a community. Social media has recognized this by encouraging people to build or identify a "profile" — a face they present to the world — and to join "groups" and "networks" and make "friends." This vocabulary is an everyday tool nowadays for most people born after 1985.[3] You've probably noticed that often young adults can be together in the same room and yet also connected to conversations on smartphones and computers with the world outside the room. Older adults may deplore this, but it is actually a condition of people's lives now. It is possible to be in constant contact with a wide variety of voices. But many young adults I've talked to also express a desire for ways to be present to one another "in the room" (even if it is a Zoom room!). Some even suggest that this ability to be present to others is a skill they fear they are losing.

What you may crave is what Parks calls a "hearth" — a place of community and safety where you can rest from the challenges of the surrounding culture, which so importantly shapes early adulthood, and be fully yourself with a group of trusted friends and mentors, in a safe and welcoming place. The materials provided here are designed to guide the conversation for groups of young adults gathered around whatever hearth the church provides for them, as they explore their own approaches to the task of shaping a faithful life. But they can also be used for an individual process of discernment, with invitations to write for personal reflection or to guide a conversation with a friend or a mentor.

The Shape of this Workbook

Shaping a Faithful Life provides a framework for young adults to explore six key questions that can help them make the connections between faith and practice that shape a meaningful life, drawing on the resources of Christian tradition. If you use it in a group, you can just agree to work through this book together, with time in between for individual reflection, or you may work with a facilitator, using additional resources provided electronically. Following is a summary of the steps in this process.

In session I, the concept of discernment is introduced, as a practice that invites us not so much to seek answers as to ask questions in the context of a life of faith. Six basic reflection questions are introduced in this session, and session I focuses on the first two questions. The questions are:

- *The Profile Question*: What do you "do"? How do you answer this question at a social gathering (how do you describe your professional or "public" identity)? This may or may not be closely related to the next question.
- *The Purpose Question*: What is your "real work"? Or, to put it another way, what work, when you are doing it, makes you feel that you are most fully and truly yourself?
- *The Passion Question* is the focus of session II: In the world of work, community, and relationships where you find yourself, what do you feel must change? This question invites you to explore a vision for the world—what writers including Verna Dozier, Desmond Tutu, and Michael Curry have called the "dream of God" for a particular situation.
- *The People Question*, in session III, looks at relationships and community, and offers a structure for engaging in discernment with a group of people through a "clarity team"—a time-limited process based on the Quaker practice of the "clearness committee."
- *The Practice Question*, the focus of session IV, asks about the activities or practices you engage in to help you live a life that matches your values around time, money, relationships, and the needs of others.
- *The Prayer Question*, in session V, introduces two broadly defined approaches to prayer that I classify as "showing up" prayers and "paying attention" prayers. Two guided meditations invite you to experience these approaches to prayer.

Session VI uses poetry and some personal storytelling to offer some fresh images of vocation and invite you to reflect further on how you have experienced God's call over the course of your life so far.

Session VII gathers our emerging responses to all these questions and explores how discernment informs a life of discipleship. Using scripture and several approaches to a life review, this closing session will challenge you to begin constructing a "rule of life"—a simple set of practices that will help you to continue to listen to God's presence and call in your life going forward.

Each session includes an invitation to Bible study, a time to delve into one or more of the discernment questions, and one or more invitations to practice, including some classic practices that have shaped the Christian tradition for centuries and are being reclaimed in our time.

The chapters that follow are labeled "sessions" because I imagine them as time that a reader may spend either alone or, ideally, with a group.

Finally, I want to note that young adults are *adults*, and that many of the materials and practices offered here can be adapted to other ages and stages of adult life, or even used in intergenerational groups.

SESSION I

Profile and Purpose

Heavenly Father and mother, friend and lover of our souls,in you we live and move and have our being. We humbly pray you, so to guide and govern us by your Holy Spirit, that in all the cares and occupations of our lives we may not forget you, but remember that we are ever walking in your sight; through Christ our Lord. Amen. (Adapted from the Book of Common Prayer 100)

The words *vocation* and *discernment* have an institutional ring for many of us. In the Episcopal Church, as in other mainline denominations, these words have been associated particularly with clergy, and with the question of whether someone is called to ordained ministry in the church. But part of our purpose here is to reclaim these words as part of a long Christian tradition that belongs to everyone, regardless of one's position within the church. Vocation, as its Latin root suggests, is about God's calling in our lives, and the stories in the gospels of Jesus calling his disciples give us some clues about what this looks like. The idea of vocation is based on confidence in a God who desires good for the world and for each of us, and wants each of us to participate in the work of reconciliation and healing in the world, "according to the gifts given us" (The Book of Common Prayer catechism 855; Romans 12:6). Everyone has a vocation.

1

Vocation or, Better, Calling

In his book *Wishful Thinking*, Frederick Buechner names well the experience of God's call in our time:

> There are all different kinds of voices calling you to all different kinds of work, and the problem is to find out which is the voice of God rather than Society, say, or the Superego, or Self-Interest. By and large a good rule for finding out is this: the kind of work God usually calls you to is the kind of work (a) that you need most to do and (b) that the world most needs to have done. If you really get a kick out of your work, you've presumably met requirement (a), but if your work is writing cigarette ads, the chances are you've missed requirement (b). On the other hand, if your work is being a doctor in a leper colony, you have probably met requirement (b), but if most of the time you're bored or depressed by it, the chances are you have not only bypassed (a), but probably aren't helping your patients much either. Neither the hair shirt nor the soft berth will do. The place God calls you to is the place where your deep gladness and the world's deep hunger meet.[4]

"Your deep gladness" — your heart's desire — and "the world's deep hunger" meet somewhere, and that is where we find our purpose, our calling or vocation. All discernment is grounded in seeking our deepest desire, believing as we do that God speaks in our hearts and through our deepest yearnings. Your particular way of being a disciple flows from who you are. A foundation of discernment is knowing who we are, right where we are now — not who we hope to be later, but who we are at this moment in life. For many younger adults, swept up in a culture that is always trying to tell us what we want or should want, this first step — getting in touch with our true desire — can be the most challenging, and the most freeing.

Kathleen Cahalan offers another way into the whole question of vocation and discernment for everyone in her book *The Stories We Live*. She frames the book around the different ways that God calls us. "We are called," she writes,

> To be Followers of Christ
> As We are
> From People, Places, Situations

For Service and Work
Through Each Other
In Suffering
By the God WITHIN.[5]

As you think about your own sense of calling, look over this list. Is there one of these prepositions that seems particularly relevant to where you are right now in your life? Sit with this phrase and spend five minutes just reflecting or freewriting the thoughts that it raises in you. Do this over several days and see what emerges.

Many of us have experienced a sense of call, perhaps without recognizing it. It can come as a desire for change and rededication of life for God's purposes, even though we may not express this in theological language. Sometimes it is a perception that there is a job to be done that urgently needs doing; we are hearing some modern-day equivalent of "Whom shall I send, and who will go for us?" (Isaiah 6:8), and we just want to say, "Here am I, send me!" But we may not know where to go from there. Often people report a sense of restlessness, a sense that "God is trying to tell me something, and I don't quite know what it is." Buechner and Cahalan provide some useful sorting out for this. You may find it helpful to return to their language, in its full context, as we go through this process of shaping a faithful life.

Discernment is the practice of attending to the action and presence of God the Holy Spirit in our lives. To get a sense of discernment as experience, try this: In a darkened room, light a candle (I sometimes do this if I am up very early and waiting for the dawn). In the dark, we gradually discern what is there to see by using the little light we have. We see by means of light, which means that light is always around us. But how often do we actually notice the light and how it is working? Usually, we need the help of an artist or photographer to show us the light. When we're in the dark about the meaning and purpose of our lives, discernment can help focus our attention on the light: the presence and action of God in our lives, using practices of prayer, stories from our faith tradition, and guiding questions.

When we talk about vocation and call, we often associate it with questions about the future: Should I go to grad school or get a job? How will I make my living? What plans for the future will give meaning and purpose to my life? There are many stories of call throughout scripture (I provide a list of them at the end of this book), but the thing to notice about the way Jesus calls his disciples in the gospels is that it's not about the future, it's about right now.

Practice 1: Bible Study

The approach to Bible study that this book will be taking is summed up in one of the prayers in the Book of Common Prayer, and it's a good prayer to use whenever you are settling in to study a passage from the Bible:

> Blessed Lord, who caused all holy Scriptures to be written for our learning: Grant us so to hear them, read, mark, learn and inwardly digest them, that we may embrace and ever hold fast the blessed hope of everlasting life, which you have given us in our Savior Jesus Christ . . .
> (The Book of Common Prayer 236)

I love this phrase "for our learning" because it suggests that whether we are new to a passage from the Bible or have heard it many times before, there is always something more to learn, because we believe that the Holy Spirit speaks to us through the stories, experiences, images, and ideas recorded in scripture. Though these texts come from very different historical and cultural contexts from our own, we come to them with the expectation that there is something here for us. And we learn by reading, by "marking" — paying attention to those words or ideas that stop or puzzle us, and by "inwardly digesting" — using our imagination, memory, and life experiences to make sense of the stories as they come to us on this reading.

With this approach in mind, read the story of Jesus calling his first disciples as we encounter it in the Gospel of Mark. The gospels are the first four books of the New Testament, and each one tells the story of Jesus's life and teaching, in a slightly different way, for a different audience of early Christians. Even though Matthew is the first gospel in our Bibles, most scholars believe that the gospel of Mark was the earliest to be written down. It is dated around 60–70 CE, a generation after Jesus's death and resurrection. Mark's gospel emphasizes the importance of faith by portraying Jesus's disciples as failing to understand the truth about Jesus while they were with him. In Mark, things happen quickly. The word "immediately" appears forty-one times in this gospel, and this story is about an immediate response to Jesus's call. Look at this story as it is told in Mark. I'm quoting it here in the Revised Standard Version (RSV) because there's something about the translation here that's closer to the original Greek than more recent, inclusive-language translations, and important for our purposes.

> And passing along by the Sea of Galilee, he saw Simon and Andrew the brother of Simon casting a net in the sea for they were fishermen. And Jesus said to them, "Follow me and I will make you fishers of men." And immediately they left their nets and followed him.
>
> Mark 1:16–18 RSV

"They were fishermen" and Jesus promises to make them "fishers of men." The phrase is a familiar one for people used to the Revised Standard and King James Versions of the Bible, and some of us may have heard it quoted before. But what does this mean?

In *Lamb*, a comic novel based on the life of Jesus and his friends, novelist Christopher Moore portrays the young Jesus, Joshua, as an effective but often clueless Messiah who needs to rely often on the practical advice of his childhood friends, especially the narrator, Biff, and their friend Maggie (Mary Magdalene). In Moore's rendering of this story, these disciples overhear Jesus calling Simon and Andrew to be "fishers of men" and Maggie explodes, "What the hell does *that* mean!" They advise Joshua that the "fishers of men" thing isn't working for people. But a few pages later, Biff tries to recruit two oarlock makers by saying, "Come follow us and you can be oarlock-makers-of men." Seeing their puzzlement, he turns to Joshua and says, "See? It doesn't make sense!"[6]

Biff's riff on the phrase "fishers of men" actually makes more sense than he admits. The original Greek in this passage states that "they were fishermen"—that's their profession, part of who they were. Jesus's call literally translates "Follow me" (do as I do; model your lives after mine) and I will "make you to become fishers-for-people." His call is about a transformation, from what they were to a new version of who they are. Though they leave their nets behind, there's continuity between who these disciples are in the now and who they're being called to become. Notice that they are not given a job description. They are not told what will happen in the future if they take this step. The invitation is simply, "Follow me." It is valuable, in practicing discernment, to begin where we are—whether we are fishermen, or oarlock-makers, or whatever we consider ourselves to be right now—paying attention to what difference the call of Jesus might make.

Practice 2: Going Deeper

As a way to begin where you are, spend some time reflecting on these six questions. Don't overthink it. Set aside about 15 minutes as just a first run-through. We will be returning to these questions throughout the journey of *Shaping a Faithful Life* to help us explore vocation in the NOW: Profile, Purpose, Passion, People, Practice, Prayer. These six questions will frame our exploration process of shaping a faithful life.

Start by thinking through these questions on your own. You may want to "freewrite"—just putting down on paper whatever comes to you. Or read through the questions and then take a short walk or settle into a place where you feel comfortable and content, and reflect on your response to these questions. After you've had time to reflect, share your responses with a friend or a small group, in person or online, listening also for what you can learn from other people's answers to these questions.

The Profile Question: What do you do? How do you answer this question at a social gathering (how do you describe your professional or public identity)? What is the face you present to the world, and how does that connect to your sense of identity?

_____

_____

_____

_____

_____

_____

_____

_____

The Purpose Question: What is your real work, or, to put it another way, What do you most enjoy doing? What is it that, when you are doing it, makes you feel that you are most fully and truly yourself? Many adults do not yet know the answer to this question, but the process of asking it, with a group that is listening carefully, can be helpful in exploring your values and motivations.

_____

_____

_____

_____

_____

_____

_____

_____

_____

The Passion Question: In the world of work, community, and relationships where you find yourself, what do you feel must change? Where in your daily life or work do you want to shake your fists and cry out in frustration, "SOMETHING must be done about _____?"

_____

_____

_____

_____

_____

_____

_____

The People Question: Who are the people whose voices guide you in your spiritual life? Where do you hear the voice of God in your human relationships right now? What might be missing in those relationships?

_____

_____

_____

_____

_____

_____

_____

_____

The Practice Question: What activities or practices do you engage in to help you live a life that matches your deepest values about time, money, relationships, and the needs of others? What about your own need to stay grounded in what you most deeply believe? Does anything seem to be missing or out of balance in these practices?

_____

_____

_____

_____

_____

_____

_____

_____

_____

_____

The Prayer Question: How do you pray? Where in your daily life and work have you been most often or most clearly aware of the presence of God? How do you respond to this awareness?

_____

_____

_____

_____

_____

_____

_____

_____

_____

Make some notes, or talk to a friend or a small group about your responses to these questions: Which question was hardest for you? Which seemed easiest? What surprised you as you went through these questions?

_____

_____

_____

_____

_____

_____

_____

_____

_____

Practice 3: Profile and Purpose

Having looked through all of these questions in a preliminary way, let's pause over the first two: the profile question and the purpose question. In his now-classic book *Falling Upward*, Richard Rohr has suggested that we spend what he calls the first half of life building the "container" for who we are really created and called to be. The tasks of early adulthood — finding work to make a living, committing to relationships, forming a household of one's own — all of these belong to this first half of life.[7] They can become so consuming that larger questions of meaning and purpose can begin to seem like a luxury. For this reason, I like to invite people to place in dialogue the profile question and the purpose question.

What is your profile? If you have ever constructed a resume or a cover letter, or set up a social media presence, you have addressed the profile question: What is the part of yourself you present to the world?

I have always found the profile question a challenging one, especially in social situations. In the highly professional and high-pressure world I have inhabited in the Washington, DC area, there is often an unspoken expectation that vocational identity should match what I do for a living. What I *do* is supposed to reflect who I *am*. But for many of us who have taken vocational questions seriously, this is a false, even damaging, expectation. That's why I separate the profile question and the purpose question.

There can be depths behind our response to that "What do you do?" question. I remember a social situation, traveling in Europe with my scientist-husband, where I found myself making polite conversation with a postdoctoral student. When he asked me the inevitable, "So, what do you do?" I paused over what I might say: "I'm a poet?" "I'm an academic working in literature and theology?" "I teach at a seminary and offer one-on-one spiritual counseling to people." For some reason I chose this last response, and his reaction was telling. He stepped back, stared at me in amazement, and said, "So, you're a believer!" By the time I came up with a response beyond "Yes!" he had moved on, but the conversation reminded me that my answer to the profile question can blend into naming a sense of purpose, and sometimes in unexpected ways.

Sometimes the purpose question eludes us until we face a crisis, and it is more common than we like to think for people in their twenties and thirties to come to a crisis where they have to deal with a major loss, or a health or financial crisis, even though we tend to associate these things with later parts of life. Because of my own life experience, I've had occasion to listen to the stories of people who received a cancer diagnosis in their twenties and thirties and learned how often a crisis experience can break open our early notions of what our profile and purpose in life might be.[8]

I was in my late thirties when my own struggles to answer the profile question came up against the purpose question in a way that was almost comical. At 37, when both my children were under the age of 6, I was diagnosed with early-stage breast cancer. Completely unexpected, in the midst of a busy life where I took health for granted, this diagnosis felt to me like a terrifying and sudden encounter with my own mortality. It shook me, even though I was assured that at the stage it was found, the disease was curable with surgery—the standard of care at the time. And this proved to be true.

The profile question turned up weirdly when I was lying on the operating table, still awake as the surgery team was preparing to administer anesthesia. The doctors and nurses were making light conversation (to observe the effects of the medicine), and one of the nurses asked me, brightly, "So, what do you do, Mrs. S.?" At the time I was an unemployed academic, with a Ph.D. from a prestigious university and an unfinished scholarly book in the works, and most of my time was spent at home with my two young children. So, the profile question was a touchy one, but the answer that came out of me, at that liminal moment, was this: "I'm a mom." Although the question she asked was "What do you do?" the question I was answering was "What are you living for?" What is it that will make it worthwhile to save your life at this moment? What is your sense of purpose, even call? The answer was clear.

That wasn't where the nurse wanted to go, so she asked the question again ("What else do you do, outside your home?"), and now it got complicated. She was staying at the profile level, so, partly befuddled, I played along. I said something about my doctoral dissertation and poetry, and one of the doctors quipped, "Oh, I like some poetry, but not those Romantics like Keats and Shelley." "I wrote my dissertation partly on Shelley," I told him, as the room exploded in laughter at the doctor's expense. But he caught my eye just before I went under, and I realized he had heard my first answer, "I'm a mom," and he knew what I was living for.

If you have faced any kind of crisis in early adulthood, you may be able to tell a story, too, about the surface answer—the profile answer—and what actually lies beneath it. Sometimes you find that the meeting of your deep gladness and the world's deep need that Buechner describes is right there, when you really look at your answers to these questions. Sometimes this exercise will expose some restlessness. Always these questions offer a way of attending to where you are right now, as you begin to reflect on God's call in your life.

What I Remember

The deep truth is imageless. (Shelley)

The operating room door has shut behind me.
   My clothes are in a locker.
   There's a nametag on my arm to remind them who I am.
I lie on the table in the bright, normal light
   Of other people's morning routine.
A nurse asks me, brightly, if I know the date and day.
   ("The patient always knows the date," she tells her trainee, knowingly).
We chat routinely, and I am brave
   Almost forgetting what we are here to do
      To save my life
         ("Total" . . . "simple". . . . the release form said).
"What do you do?" Another nurse asks
   And I answer with the deep truth:
     "I'm a Mom."
"Oh," she goes on, politely inquiring
   About ages, and sexes, and grades in school.
Then: "But what <u>else</u> do you do, outside your home?"
   More chit-chat, even laughing, about "what else"
     —teaching and writing, dissertations, (Shelley!)

   But I have given
        my answer.

The last thing I remember, against the routine cheer
   A doctor's eyes, above his mask
     stricken with humanity[9]

Think back to Jesus calling the fishermen: "They were fishermen." What aspect of where you are right now seems alive and important to you as you consider how Jesus may be calling you at this time in your life? If it is a muddle, note the muddle. We will be circling back to these questions and the additional questions they raise in future exercises and meetings.

Look back at the profile and purpose questions that you've been working with and write some thoughts or share with a friend or a small group.

_____

_____

_____

_____

_____

_____

_____

_____

_____

_____

_____

_____

_____

_____

_____

_____

_____

_____

Practice 4: From the Tradition: A Way into Centering Prayer

All major world religions have practices of meditation connected to them, and Christianity is no exception, though until recently this tradition was not widely taught in churches. Centering or contemplative prayer is a way of quieting down so that we can fully be where we are in the present moment, open and receptive to the Spirit already within us. It helps us enter into what the Anglican writer Evelyn Underhill has called "that deep place where the soul is at home with God."[10]

Prominent teachers of centering prayer, including Thomas Keating and Cynthia Bourgeault,[11] offer different ways into this practice, but here are some basics:

- It is best for any ongoing prayer practice to have a particular place that you return to when it is time to pray. This already begins to signal to the mind that it is time to quiet down. You may want to light a candle, or have an icon or prayer beads, or a plant or lovely piece of fabric, to mark your space.
- Begin by settling into a comfortable position where you are not distracted by your body's physical position. Most people find it helps to have your feet on the floor, and your spine straight and supported, but some like to pray lying down or sitting on the floor, against the wall. Do whatever works for you.
- Pay attention to your breathing. Take five deep breaths, and as you breathe in, be aware of God's love surrounding you. As you breathe out, be conscious of breathing out any distractions or worries or churning thoughts that may have come with you into your prayer time.
- Now, as you breathe quietly, be aware of the divine presence around you and within you. As distractions emerge, simply notice and dismiss them. The first few times people try praying this way they often find the distractions overwhelming and conclude that they can't do it, but the process of noticing and releasing distractions or concerns can also become a way into a deeper prayer that is beyond thoughts or words.

John Main teaches a version of this kind of prayer that invites you to choose a "prayer word" that you will always use when you come to centering prayer.[12] The word is meant to be an interior focal point—a place you come back to when distractions arise.

The heart of this prayer is a simply sitting and waiting on God. If you are new to it, try setting a timer for a short period of time—10 minutes at most—and just be with the practice for that length of time. You can lengthen the time set aside for this prayer as you find yourself desiring it. Many people also find it a rich experience to practice this way of prayer in a centering prayer group—sometimes beginning with an intention that we bring before God, as we then release our own fuss and concern into the depths of the Divine Presence.

Many of the exercises in this book invite you to begin the way I have described the beginning of centering prayer, by attending to your breathing and the presence and love of God that you take in with each breath. Even if this isn't your preferred way of prayer, it may have something to teach you.

SESSION II

The Passion Question

O God of unchangeable power and eternal light: Look favorably on your whole Church, that wonderful and sacred mystery; by the effectual working of your providence, carry out in tranquility the plan of salvation; let the whole world see and know that things which were cast down are being raised up, and things which had grown old are being made new, and that all things are being brought to their perfection by him through whom all things were made, your Son Jesus Christ our Lord; who lives and reigns with you, in the unity of the Holy Spirit, one God, forever and ever. (The Book of Common Prayer 280)

I like to use this prayer whenever I introduce a group to the practice of discernment in Christian community. It speaks across denominations, to many aspects of the Christian life. It is about the Church, the community of faithful people, as an agent of transformation, and about the people in the Church—us—being called to transformation. Those who use the Episcopal Church's Book of Common Prayer will encounter this prayer in the Good Friday service, right after we have offered the "solemn collects," praying for the whole world, in all its brokenness and suffering. The series of prayers culminates in this one, with its declaration of hope that "things which were cast down are being raised up, and things which had grown old are being made new." It appears in the service for the Great Vigil of Easter, right after we have retold the whole history of salvation, and right before we baptize new Christians and renew our own baptismal covenant, in anticipation of the Easter feast. It is offered at ordinations and other events around the mission and ministry of the Church.

At the heart of this prayer is a petition for ongoing discernment and revelation: *Let the whole world see and know* that things which were cast down are being raised up, and things which had grown old are being made new. The prayer for the Church reminds us that we are a part of something that God is doing. The heart of Christian faith is the belief that God works in and through human beings, bringing life out of death, and empowering us to do Christ's work of reconciliation in the world.

In session I, we looked at the ways that God calls us right where we are, focusing especially on the profile and purpose questions—the work we are doing now that God comes to transform, deepen, and call us beyond. Now we turn to the passion question: What is it that makes you want to clench your fists with urgency and say, "This must change, NOW." If you feel anger or frustration or grief about the issues that arouse your passion, you are, in a way, sharing in God's heart. An important step toward faithfulness in our lives is to recognize that the world is not the way it is meant to be, that there is a better way that a loving God intended for us and for all of Creation, all of Society. It can be painful to share that vision, seeing how far we fall short, but that is part of the invitation as we seek to shape a faithful life.

When Christians pray the Lord's Prayer, the prayer that Jesus taught his disciples, we say, "Thy kingdom come, thy will be done." What do we mean by that? In Jesus's time the image of God as a benign monarch, a ruler who knew what was best for people, was one that people could access readily. This image of God took root in sometimes destructive ways for the many centuries that Christianity was the dominant religion of the ruling powers. In our time, we have what most of us see as a reasonable distrust of absolute power, so the idea of a kingdom does not have the resonance it has had at other times in biblical tradition and Christian history. How might we better express that consent to a divine purpose suggested in *thy kingdom come*?

Brian McLaren, among others, has proposed that instead of using kingdom language or even gender neutral "reign of God" language, we invite imagination into the picture, and imagine God as having a vision or a dream for our human life, one that we are constantly called to live into. "The call to faith," writes McLaren, "is the call to trust God and God's dreams enough to realign our dreams with God's, to dream our little dreams within God's big dream."[13]

The prophetic writer Verna Dozier writes of the dream of God as a persistent "call to return" to the path of justice and wholeness that God originally intended for God's people, and she encourages all Christians to learn the story of scripture. In that story, despite moments of terrible brokenness, we can discern a persistent call to wholeness that God never abandons.

If we read the whole, overarching story of scripture we can begin to see that it is a story about who God wants to be for God's people. It is a story of God's dream for human life. It is a vision of humanity created in the image of God, to be companions and collaborators with God in the shaping of a harmonious and beautiful Creation. This session invites you to "dream with God," to use your imagination in a prayerful way, in awareness of the whole biblical story of a God who desires good things for us. This requires us to confront brokenness in our world and in our lives.

In her classic book, *The Dream of God*, Dozier[14] emphasizes the narrative arc of scripture as the context for reading any part of it. If you look at the whole story, she insists, you find that it a story about who God wants to be for God's people. It is, in fact, a story of God's dream for human life, a vision of humanity as created in the image of God, to be companions and collaborators with God in the shaping of a harmonious and beautiful Creation. Human faithlessness may thwart this dream, but God persists.

Here's how Dozier summarizes the story: It begins with the creation of a world that God called "good," continuing with the gift of the Garden of Eden and humanity's failure to stay there on God's terms. It continues with the calling of Abraham to be a blessing to the world, and the story of his descendants. It's a human story, with ups and downs, shocking sinfulness, and violence. Through it all there is a God who keeps calling people back to a deeper dream of freedom and abundant life. In Exodus, with its story of liberation led by Moses, we see a God who cares about the ordering of our common life and who desires justice even more than worship. Subsequent books of the Bible tell of the people's struggle to keep the covenant, God's promise to sustain them as a holy people, living into God's love for the world. Ultimately when the people's failings result in the Babylonian exile, those exiled sing of the hope of restoration, and in the overarching narrative, God keeps this promise.

The vision of a God who desires our good, yet leaves us free, is continued in the New Testament, with the coming of Jesus, whose crucifixion shows how far human society, religious institutions, and culture have fallen from the message of justice, peace, and love that is at the heart of God. Jesus's resurrection, the founding event of Christianity, tells us that this message cannot ultimately be defeated, and that is the hope we carry, through all the complexities and distortions and abuses of human history—including the twisting and co-opting of the very story of scripture we're talking about.

Practice 1: Retelling the Whole Story

Verna Dozier challenges every Christian to tell the story of scripture in their own words, in 10 minutes or less. Think about how you might do this, touching on favorite moments in the whole story. If you don't feel you can do it yet, pay attention to stories that move you, as you hear and read them as part of this study, and see how they fit into the whole story. Here is my own current retelling of the story of scripture, inspired by Dozier's own reading and leading us back to the theme of discernment.

In the beginning, humanity was created in the image of God. We were given life and our place in Creation. The fable-story of Adam and Eve, as told in Genesis, seems to be about their failure to go along with God's plan, and their succumbing to the desire to be gods themselves. They reject their proper place in the network of Creation, as beloved creatures with a special relationship to their Creator, called and enabled to collaborate with our Creator in shaping and enhancing the abundant life that we watch being created, a life pronounced "good" in the opening chapters of Genesis.

The banishment from the Garden of Eden, and the early stories of people rebelling against God and being punished, seem to culminate in the call of Abraham in Genesis, called out from his homeland to become the father of a great people. What we sometimes forget about the call of Abraham is that his people are set apart for a special purpose that serves not just their tribe, but the whole human world. "You shall be a blessing," God says to Abraham, "and in you all the families of the earth shall be blessed" (Genesis 12:3).[15] Right from the beginning, the People of God, the descendants of Abraham, are called to be part of God's purpose for a healed and blessed world. The unfolding of this purpose ultimately drives the narrative of the Bible.

Enslaved in Egypt, the People of God are led back to freedom by Moses, a leader who is called by God to bring them to a new place, and to renew the covenant between God and the people. "You will be my people, and I will be your God," is the promise. The Torah, the Law of God, received from God through Moses, is understood as God's gift to the people—the divine expression of loving kindness, from a God who has a stake in the life of the whole Creation. Living according to the Covenant, through the spiritual and economic practices commanded there, the People of God learn a manner of living intended for fullness of life and right relationships in the human community—including the just distribution of wealth and a habit of trusting God. At the beginning, the Law is seen not as bondage and rigidity, but as a way of freedom, assuring justice in human society and communion between God and God's people.

Of course, we know how the story goes, in ongoing cycles of forgetting and returning to this fundamental relationship between humanity and God. The guiding Law and a Covenant, offered as a way to freedom and justice in human life, harden into the tools of a ruling class and religious hierarchy; prophets are ignored; wisdom cries out in the streets and is not heard (Proverbs 1:20–29).

The Christian story proclaims that this persistent love of God, longing to call humanity back to wholeness and freedom, is finally expressed in the Incarnation and passion of Jesus—in God joining us in our human lives and suffering—all that the world can do to a humanity fully dedicated to the dream of God. The cross points to the infinite, long-suffering love of this God; and the resurrection of Jesus and the sending of the Holy Spirit tell us that the dream persists, and that we, as God's people living on this side of the resurrection, are called to carry it on, despite the obstacles that we may encounter. To paraphrase one of the eucharistic prayers of the Episcopal Church, this is a God who "again and again calls us to return" (The Book of Common Prayer 370).

Within this story, we are invited to discernment, the practice of seeing the world, even a broken world, through the eyes of a loving God. For this we need imagination—a creative, lively willingness to "dream with God." Our God loves us and desires to restore us and all Creation to wholeness, but works through human action and human freedom, and desires to heal us and save us (the Greek word translated "salvation" in the New Testament, *sozo*, is about healing or "making whole"). We need to look squarely and compassionately at whatever is broken in our world and imagine our way through and beyond the brokenness, to discern "God's dream" for this situation.

Practice 2: Bible Study

A pivotal story in Hebrew scripture is the exile into Babylon. According to biblical tradition, the conquest of Israel by the Babylonians, and the exile of large numbers of Israelite people to Babylon in 522 BCE, comes as a result of centuries of faithlessness by the rulers and the people who fail to honor the Covenant, worshipping foreign gods and neglecting the needs of the poor. The biblical writers note that this happens despite repeated warnings from the prophets. Ultimately, God, in grief, punishes them through the hands of the Chaldeans (another name for the rulers of Babylon), taking them into exile. When their time in exile is fulfilled, they are invited home. That's how the story is told, about a particularly painful time in the people's history.

This passage at the end of 2 Chronicles tells the whole story of exile and return in one chapter, with lurid evocations of the suffering of those massacred and captured, and with lamentation over a loss that has come upon the people because of their faithlessness. Striking in this story is not only the harshness of what the story depicts as inevitable suffering ("there was no remedy"), but also the grief of the God who watches it happen and seeks to call the people home. Here is the story as told at the end of 2 Chronicles. Listen to this story read aloud or read it slowly on your own. Pay attention to your feelings at each point in the story. Imagine the experience of the various generations in this story. What difference does it make to tell their story in this way, as part of a pattern of fall, exile, and return?

> The LORD, the God of their ancestors, sent persistently to them by his messengers, because he had compassion on his people and on his dwelling place; but they kept mocking the messengers of God, despising his words, and scoffing at his prophets, until the wrath of the LORD against his people became so great that there was no remedy. Therefore he brought up against them the king of the Chaldeans, who killed their youths with the sword in the house of their sanctuary and had no compassion on young man or young woman, the aged or the feeble; he gave them all into his hand. All the vessels of the house of God, large and small, and the treasures of the house of the LORD, and the treasures of the king and of his officials, all these he brought to Babylon. They burned the house of God, broke down the wall of Jerusalem, burned all its palaces with fire, and

destroyed all its precious vessels. He took into exile in Babylon those who had escaped from the sword, and they became servants to him and to his sons until the establishment of the kingdom of Persia, to fulfill the word of the LORD by the mouth of Jeremiah, until the land had made up for its Sabbaths. All the days that it lay desolate it kept Sabbath, to fulfill seventy years.

In the first year of King Cyrus of Persia, in fulfillment of the word of the LORD spoken through Jeremiah, the LORD stirred up the spirit of King Cyrus of Persia so that he sent a herald throughout all his kingdom and also declared in a written edict: "The LORD, the God of heaven, has given me all the kingdoms of the world, and he has charged me to build him a house at Jerusalem, which is in Judah. Whoever is among you of all his people, may the LORD his God be with him. Let him go up."

2 Chronicles 36:15–23

The edict of Cyrus of Persia, coming at the end of 2 Chronicles and again at the beginning of the book of Ezra, sounds a voice of promise from a God who does not give up on God's people. This is a moment of hope and joyful return in the life of the People of God—a moment in their story that holds up belief in a God who keeps faith and perpetually calls the people home. But there are many other moments in this summary of the whole story of exile and return, and those moments were violent, painful, and apparently hopeless for those who were living through them.

Practice 3: Guided Meditation: An Imaginative Invitation to Dream with God through Poetry

Here, then, is the question at the heart of discernment: What is God's dream for me, and how does that dream connect with God's larger dream? Some years ago, I found myself creating a long poem that really invited me to participate imaginatively in the dream of God. The inspiration began in the Christmas season when I was the reader of the first lesson in the traditional service of *Nine Lessons and Carols*. The first lesson is the story of the "fall." Some of my family members have wondered why we read this troubling story on Christmas Eve, but I find that in the context of the whole story, it is a blessing to remember that the story of God coming to us in the Incarnation begins with this initial moment of utterly broken relationship, and the heartbreak is a divine one. Reading this passage in the service, I remember being struck especially by the image of God coming back to the garden in the evening, anticipating a companionable visit with Adam and Eve. The way the story is told, God is shocked by Adam and Eve hiding in the garden and by their shame, and there is a poignancy in God's pleading question, when the whole story of the serpent, and their disobedience, comes out.

So, as I walked in the woods the following spring, the closing lines of this now longish poem came to me, and I realized I was being invited to write a poem in the voice of God, hearing those musings as God walked in the garden. What emerged was a series of images for the dream of God, and I offer you this poem as a prompt to your own meditation.

The Anglican spiritual writer Evelyn Underhill writes that the secret of a faithful life is "To stand beside the generous Creative Love, maker of all things visible and invisible, including those we do not like, and see them with the eyes of the Artist Lover."[16] Read it aloud, or better, listen to it read aloud and pay attention to the images of the world as God desires it to be. What are your feelings at the end of this poem?

In the Cool of the Evening
Every evening I come here, and draw you to my breast
    What have you noticed today?
I am waiting to hear, for everything you find
    Is fresh and new to you, never seen this way before.
As you tell me about it, Creation grows richer.
And we celebrate together
    In heart's joy and dancing,
        Here in this garden
        In the cool of the evening.

Have you noticed
    How the tiny white violets open to the sun
    and close at evening?

Have you tasted the freshness of ripened grapes, or berries,
fresh from the vine
　Or smelled
　　Tell me what you have smelled!
Have you been to the sea's shore yet, and have you noticed
　How smoothly the sandpipers skim before the waves
Or how the pelican hovers, then lets go and plunges—sinking her
heart into the sea, where she is fed?
Have you heard the sea swell pound and seen the
　　　　Waves crest, pink in the sunrise?

Have you noticed yet
A pulsing beat, all through you
This is life:
　　　My gift to you.

And as each day there is evening and there is morning
So you will know
　　　the ebb and flow of this great pulse.
When it is filling you, you will be strong and eager
　And run out to me boldly
　And leap for joy.

And sometimes this force of life will wane in you
　and you will know
It is time to rest with me awhile.
And I will be glad to welcome you here.

So there will be
　mornings and evenings,
turnings and passages, and I in all of them.

I am waiting to hear of the first time you notice
The trembling joy of bodies meeting,
　flesh touching flesh.
And how in that union, everything joins and dances, and dances,
and dances.

It is not good
    That you should be alone.
I will make more of you
    more of you, yet out of you
Each new person will be part of one before,
    Yet also new,
        glorious, separate.
So each of you will be
        one flesh with all the others
And all will be one body with the earth that brought you forth.

And as in one another
You see yourselves, and not yourselves
So each new meeting, each new friendship,
Will carry in it more of me
As in each new person, each new way of love
    I come again among you.

When you feel a new life growing within you
    Sharing your flesh, swimming and frolicking
    held within you, and a part of you.
You will know, from the nearness of this growing life
How I am bound to you, and each of you to me.
Wait until you see
    the tiny toes and fingers
The fresh-born miracle of a new child
    As now you come to me
each evening, for food and loving
So the children will come to you, and you will know
    the wonder of a fresh life
    Separate, yet of you
    Seeing more than you had noticed before.

There will be more of you, and they will find each other
And out of one another, bring forth more new lives,
and each one will be different,
    and you will love the differences!

Perhaps, when there are more of you
    You will learn to make
From all this variety of noises and voices
    Songs
And I shall be among you in the singing.

With more of you, there will be
Bodies at play, in games and dancing
You will stretch out arms and move your feet,
Turning and leaping, in patterns and figures
Pulsing to music, drumming a dance
Your bodies moving as my heart moves
Stretching and bounding, rejoicing with you.

I have made you to know it all
    Every detail of this Creation
    All that I have called "Good."

When will you learn the intricacies:
    Puzzles, numbers, patterns, shapes
The delight of randomness
The satisfaction
    Of order and equation?
I will teach you how, and as we gaze together
This living Creation, shifting and changing
    infinite in its surprises,
            will unfold.
Your bodies
    cells and systems,
The universe itself, from tiniest particles
    to unimagined vastness.
I want you to know it all
For all of it is good.

I am waiting
for the first time you bring me
    something you have made, and say,

"Look! I made this! It is for you."
And I will know your pleasure
And that you have known
   the joy of making, my deepest joy.
And so in fresh creation more will be added,
   And we will be joined:
In weaving and in making
   We will be joined.

Every evening, in the coolness, I come and walk
   and wait to see
What you have discovered
   As more and more, you wake up to the world.

I look for you now, running to me
   all aglow with news.
Come, leap to my embrace,
   Drink in my love.
      And tell me all of it.
Laughter shall spring out, and we shall watch creation grow
   And dance and feast together
   In the cool of the evening.

Come to me! Where are you?
   Why would you hide from me?

O my beloved ones
What is this
   What is this
   That you
      have done?

_____

_____

_____

_____

_____

_____

_____

_____

_____

_____

_____

One thing more about dreaming with God: it can be painful, because we fall so far short of the dream, so often. Because my poem was inspired by her work, I was honored to have a chance to read this poem to Verna Dozier, author of *The Dream of God*, toward the end of her life, and I shall always remember her response. She listened intently to each image, nodding occasionally in appreciation. When I finished reading, she solemnly and slowly repeated the last lines back to me: "O my beloved ones/What is this/that you/have done?" And I recalled her own conclusion to *The Dream of God*, where she writes of the important roles of clergy and laity in the healing work that God always desires and seeks to bring into being, the Church's call to "another way" that often seems far from the way things are. She writes:

> The people of God are called to a possibility other than the kingdoms of the world. They must be ambassadors — again, St. Paul's word — in every part of life. They witness to another way that governments can relate to one another, that money can be earned and spent, that doctors and caregivers and engineers and lawyers and teachers can serve their constituencies, that wordsmiths and musicians and artists and philosophers can give us new visions of the human condition.

All of them need the support system of the institutional church. There must be those resting places where the story is treasured and passed on in liturgy and education. There must be those islands of refuge where the wounded find healing; the confused, light; the fearful, courage; the strong, gratitude. Maintaining such institutions is the ministry of the clergy.

We have all failed the dream of God. The terribly patient God still waits.

Dozier, 1991, 150

To ground your meditation, think back to that question: What is your passion? What is the thing that makes you say, "This MUST change"? Keeping in mind the poem's vision of a God who desires good things for us, create something that communicates the healing of a place of brokenness you have identified. Don't worry about feasibility or proposing a program or solution. Just describe God's dream for this situation, as you understand it.

If you are journaling, you may choose to take one section of the poem "In the Cool of the Evening" and expand on that image and what it evokes for you. Or you may want to respond to the Vernier Dozier passage. You may do this in writing, or perhaps pick up some colored pencils or markers and create an image that reflects something from your meditation. When you have rendered your sense of the dream of God, consider sharing it with someone else.

_____

_____

_____

_____

_____

_____

_____

_____

Practice 4: From the Tradition: Imaginative Prayer in the Ignatian Tradition

Ignatius of Loyola, in his spiritual exercises, recommends attending to the imagination and the feelings you have when reflecting on stories from the Bible. Though it works with other parts of scripture, this approach is especially helpful in deepening our receptiveness to God's Word to us in passages from the gospels. Here are the basics:

- Choose your text the night before, or earlier in the day if you are praying in the evening, and read it through, so it is basically familiar when you come to meditation.
- Settle yourself. Sit comfortably, in a place that is congenial to you. Do what you need to do to quiet down and listen. Ask God to touch you through this passage from scripture. Bring into your prayer your desire to be open to God's leading.
- Compose the scene imaginatively, using your senses. Read the passage slowly and carefully, aloud if you can, several times. Invite the Holy Spirit to guide your imagination. As you read, try to enter the story imaginatively in one or more of these ways:

  1. What do you see? Hear? Smell? Who is with you? What are the surroundings? Take your time, in the story, to "compose the scene" and imagine yourself in it.
  2. Locate yourself. Who are you in the story? One of the characters listed? Someone else who must have been there? Yourself, with questions from your own life?
  3. You may find you are led to enter a conversation with Jesus or with someone else in the story, or some other image of God that comes to you. Have that conversation.

- Let your imagination take over, and let the story unfold. Be ready to be surprised at where your reflections take you, and make a conscious effort to invite the Holy Spirit.
- As you dwell with this story, ask what your feelings mean. If you are stuck, blocked, or frustrated, bring it into this prayerful conversation. Ask whatever questions come to you. Or it may happen that you simply want to sit with the impression this story makes on you, soaking in the sense of God's presence that you are experiencing. Go where you are led, trusting that whatever happens is a gift of grace.

- When you feel your awareness winding down, or you feel you have responded to God's touch in this time, complete the meditation by reciting a familiar prayer, the Lord's Prayer, a psalm, or a hymn verse.
- Give yourself time at the end of your period of meditation to "ground" what you have experienced. Write down some response, share with someone in conversation, or create something using paints, colored pencils, collage, a multimedia blog, photos, or whatever artistic medium helps you to share in the divine creativity.[17]

_____

_____

_____

_____

_____

_____

_____

_____

_____

_____

_____

_____

_____

_____

_____

_____

_____

_____

_____

SESSION III

The People Question

Almighty God, you have surrounded us with a great cloud of witnesses. Grant that we, encouraged by the people you have sent into our lives, may persevere in running the race that is set before us, knowing that we are always surrounded by a great fellowship of love and prayer. We pray in Jesus' name. (Adapted from the prayer "Of a Saint," The Book of Common Prayer 250)

We now turn to the "people" question, and I invite you to explore this question in the context of one of the richest of our traditions as Episcopalian/Anglican Christians — the Communion of Saints, who are, in a spiritual way, "our people." When I begin to think about the important people in my life, I remember the preacher of a children's sermon that drew me into the sacramental tradition of the Episcopal Church. I had been raised in a less liturgical Protestant tradition (Presbyterian), but got involved in an Episcopal church students' group when I was in college. One All Saints Sunday, the preacher reminded the children to listen to the prayer that we say before every communion service. Just before we say or sing "Holy, Holy, Holy" at communion, the celebrant says these words: "Therefore we praise you, joining our voices with angels and archangels and all the company of heaven . . ." (The Book of Common Prayer 362). Whenever you hear that prayer or whenever you feel alone, the preacher said to the congregation, "Remember the company." I treasure that sense that we are connected, through tradition and memory, to a whole company of faithful people who have gone before us. Reflecting on these words enriches my sense of connection to the communities that nurture and have nurtured me. I invite you to keep in mind that "company of heaven" as you reflect on the people question, so important to the practice of discernment.[18]

Practice 1: Bible Study: What Are You Looking for?

One of the stories of Jesus's call to the disciples invites us to look more deeply at the way we are drawn into relationship with one another and with Jesus. In session I, we considered the transformation of the fishermen to "fishers of men" in Matthew and Mark. In the Gospel of John, the story of discipleship begins with a question about discernment, as Jesus asks his would-be followers, "What are you looking for?"

> When Jesus turned and saw them following, he said to them, "What are you looking for? They said to him, "Rabbi," (which translated means Teacher), "where are you staying?" He said to them, "Come and see." They came and saw where he was staying, and they remained with him that day.
>
> John 1:38–39

The Gospel of John is remarkable for its focus on the community of disciples and their relationship with Jesus, and it is here, as well as in a later New Testament book called 1 John, that the theme of God's love for the world, expressed in Jesus, is sounded. This love is to be lived out in the Christian community, but it begins with the first disciples' relationship of love and friendship with Jesus, and his love for them. This is the version of the gospel story that focuses on God's love for the world, expressed in Jesus. (John 3:16, a verse often quoted out of context in public places, says, "For God so loved the world that he gave his only Son.") The tradition holds that the narrator of the Gospel of John is the "beloved disciple," the one who had a particularly close and intimate relationship with Jesus, and is telling this story because of that friendship. This account of the calling of the disciples marks the beginning of that friendship with Jesus, as they follow him and remain or "abide" with him that day.[19]

"What are you looking for?" At the beginning of the fourth gospel, Jesus's words invite us to hear a loving invitation to ask what we are truly looking for. What are the deepest desires of our hearts? And then to accept the invitation of Christ, to "come and see," and to remain (or abide) with him, in whatever way we are being invited to discern his presence and life in our lives at this time.

Using the imaginative reading method described in session II, try reading the story slowly, aloud, or listening to someone else reading it. As you do so, invite your imagination into your prayer. Imagine yourself as one of those disciples, on the road. You have just seen Jesus passing by and heard him named as someone having real authority. Go to him, or go to whatever your own vision of a personal God, loving, caring about you, might be, and hear Jesus call you by name: "What are you looking for?"

What are you looking for? Sit in silence with this question, and pay attention to what kinds of responses emerge. There may be nothing. You may not know what you're looking for. Sit with that. Or sit quietly and just see what surfaces. Imagine yourself, in the presence of Jesus, the Living Christ, hearing him ask you, "What are you looking for?" What is your response? What conversation might unfold from his question? What is it like for you to remain or abide with Jesus, in quiet friendship?

Practice 2: Exploring the People Question

True discernment cannot be done in isolation. We need the wisdom of community and tradition, both past and present. Archbishop Desmond Tutu writes of our interdependence with one another, named by the African word *ubuntu* – the knowledge that "I am because you are" – that our identities depend on one another.[20] Archbishop Tutu talks about how, in our interdependence with one another, our tradition speaks of being knit together with others in the body of Christ. We can learn a lot about ourselves by reflecting on the people who have shaped us. In some parts of the country, we identify ourselves by answering the question, "Who are your people?" Who are the people whose example, wisdom, challenge, and support has helped to make you who you are today? Who do you rely on to remind you that you belong to a human family beloved by God?

Write down a list of names of the people evoked by the following descriptions:

- An adult who "got" you in your childhood or young adulthood

_____

_____

- Someone (living or dead) who taught you something that gave you joy, in person or through writing, art, music, or performance

  _____

  _____

- Someone who saw in you a gift you didn't see in yourself, or affirmed what you only suspected

  _____

  _____

- Someone you turn to for wisdom

  _____

  _____

- Someone you go to when you need to "lighten up" or have fun

  _____

  _____

- Someone who listens to you/listened to you

  _____

  _____

- Someone whose example you admire (what qualities, in particular, do you admire?)

  _____

  _____

- Someone who prays for you

  _____

  _____

- Someone who has taught you something about prayer or prayer practice

_____

_____

- Someone who, when you see them, reminds you about something good in yourself

_____

_____

- Someone who is always glad to see you

_____

_____

- Someone who makes you smile whenever you see them

_____

_____

Look at your list. Imagine that you have an important decision to make in your life and you want to have help in making that decision faithfully. Circle the names of five people you would definitely want to turn to for help making that decision. What would it be like to have all of them together in the same room, listening to you? What gifts do you admire in the people you have chosen? What questions would you want to ask them? What questions would you want them to ask you?

Practice 3: The Clarity Team

We started with Jesus's question, "What are you looking for?" because discernment is about touching and identifying our deepest desires — all rooted in the desire for God that underlies our life decisions. Once we have framed a question, a community of trusted friends, all of them "on our team," rooting for our thriving, can help us, not only to weigh options (though this is helpful), but to listen for the true movements of the Holy Spirit in our hearts.

The Quakers practice a wonderful and simple way of discernment in community that they call a "clearness committee." Quaker spirituality emphasizes the inner light that each person carries. For their tradition, the practice of discernment, of learning to be open to God's leadings in our heart, becomes the whole point of life, worship, governance, and assembly. Quakers use versions of this practice even in their business meetings. Parker Palmer uses the practice of the clearness committee in his Courage Renewal program.[21]

In general, Quakers resist imposing time limits on the work of the Spirit and will work together to wait on the Spirit for however long it takes. In a concession to the general busy-ness of our lives and the structure of our programs, I am offering here a modified version of this process that you could use in the context of a small group of trusted friends. I call it the "clarity team" to emphasize especially that when we gather to help someone with discernment we are on their team. We are there to help and not to interrogate or play devil's advocate with them, but to listen with them in ways that encourage their thriving. We are "their people." Some people use a practice like this throughout their lives, assembling the same team of trusted friends with some regularity so they can access one another's wisdom and listen together for the Holy Spirit. I would love to see discernment groups or clarity teams on this model in many more of our congregations.

Here's the basic clarity team process. Select someone to be the focus person and someone to serve as the convener, and get two to four more volunteers to be listeners. If it is a very small group (five or fewer), simply choose a focus person and have everyone else be a listener, including the convener. The convener is responsible for holding the space, and especially the periods of silence between the steps in this process, so be sure the group all understands and agrees to the process before you begin.

1. Open with two minutes of prayerful silence. The convener keeps time. The convener offers, aloud, a prayer for the focus person and for the listeners, and the group's openness to the Holy Spirit. For example:

   O God of peace, you have taught us that in returning and rest we shall be saved, in quietness and in confidence shall be our strength;

by the might of your Spirit lift us, we pray, to your presence, where we may be still and know that you are God; through Jesus Christ our Lord, Amen. (The Book of Common Prayer 832)

2. The focus person (A) takes about five to ten minutes to describe a situation for which they desire the group's help for prayerful discernment. (The convener gently helps to keep A within the time limit but also encourages them to elaborate.) If possible, A will try to frame the situation as a question about God's call in their life. Listeners may ask clarifying questions at this point, not probing questions (about feelings, impressions, intuitions), but factual questions that help them understand the situation.

3. The group goes into one to three minutes of silence (the convener keeps time; this is a time for all to be opening hearts to the Holy Spirit's presence). When the silence feels deep enough, the convener may quietly indicate that anyone who would like to ask a question may begin.

4. For the next ten to twenty minutes, listeners may ask questions, and the focus person responds. Try to give everyone a chance to ask at least one question. Some listeners will have more than one question. The convener may also ask questions as they feel led. Let the Holy Spirit guide the questions and the order of listeners, but do avoid having the same person speak twice in a row. Here are some important norms for this process:

   • Listeners should avoid follow-up questions or critique. Questions are meant to help us listen for the Holy Spirit.
   • Ask open-ended questions whose answer you genuinely don't know, rather than rhetorical or yes/no questions.
   • Appropriate questions might be: How did it feel to you when _____? What was your sense of God in _____ situation? What does this situation remind you of/make you think of? What would you like/not like about this possible outcome?
   • If the listeners seem to be drifting toward a discussion, the convener may gently move the group back to prayerful listening, calling for silence.
   • Remember that the point of the group is to help the focus person reflect, in the presence of the Holy Spirit.

5. After questions subside, or when the time is up, share together another two minutes of prayerful silence.
6. The convener invites the focus person to reflect on what they have heard.
7. Ground the time together by inviting each listener to reflect on their experience of God in this session (NOT "A's situation reminded me of this experience in my life," but, "As I listened to A, I experienced/sensed/noticed . . ."). What has this time of prayer been like for you?
8. Close with silent prayer time. The convener may invite people to offer prayers silently or aloud for A or for anything that arises for them out of this time of prayerful listening. Close with the Lord's Prayer or another prayer that will "collect" these silent reflections and petitions.

The most important part of this process is the period of silence between each step. Even though it may feel awkward at first, be sure that your group observes the silence. If you are the facilitator or timekeeper, practice paying attention to your breath, and notice about how many breaths you take per minute when you are sitting calmly in silence. Use your breath to keep the time. When I lead a group, I find I take about six deep breaths, in and out, per minute, so a two-minute silence is twelve breaths. Counting my breaths rather than watching a clock also helps me to sink more deeply into silence, and also to be a little more flexible about the timing than a mechanical timer allows, though using a timer is another option. The important thing is to make sure to give time for silence in between times of conversation.

Remember, a clarity team is meant to help someone with discernment by sitting with them in the presence of God, listening together for inner leadings of the Spirit, and asking questions that will help them look at their situation. This is not a problem-solving exercise, but a way of helping someone come to greater clarity. There are no projected outcomes or answers in this process; it is all about the questions.

For your reflection: After you have worked with a clarity team either as facilitator, focus person, or listener, spend about five minutes free-writing about your experience. Write down, unedited, how you are feeling as you emerge from this process. Would you like to engage again?

Do you have a question that you would want to bring to a clarity team? What did you hear in the conversation that surprised you?

_____

_____

_____

_____

_____

_____

_____

_____

_____

_____

_____

_____

_____

_____

_____

_____

_____

_____

_____

_____

_____

_____

_____

SESSION IV

The Practice Question

Do not store up for yourselves treasures on earth, where moth and rust consume and where thieves break in and steal; but store up for yourselves treasures in heaven, where neither moth nor rust consumes and where thieves do not break in and steal. For where your treasure is, there will your heart be also.

Matthew 6:19–21

"Where your treasure is, there will your heart be also." This challenging statement invites discernment around questions about what is most important in our lives. Where is your treasure? Where is your heart? In our time these questions may be best approached by looking at what we "spend" — our time and our money.

Practice 1: Bible Study

Jesus is speaking to a long tradition in Hebrew scripture that invites people to practices that remind them of their dependence on God. In the overarching history of God's people, whenever they fall into patterns that rely on human rulers, political alliances, and the quest for riches at the expense of the poor, things do not go well. Jesus is speaking into this tradition, and in doing so he evokes a long history that his listeners would have been aware of, dating especially to the establishment of the Covenant and to the words of the prophets, notably the prophet Isaiah.

The book of Isaiah actually brings together prophetic voices from three different historical periods, reflecting on the stories of fall, exile, and return in what is often hauntingly beautiful poetry. "First Isaiah" (chapters 1–39 of Isaiah) foretells the coming of God's judgment on a series of faithless rulers and people who turn away from God. This judgment is fulfilled in the defeat of the Northern Kingdom of Israel by the Assyrian Empire and, ultimately, by the conquest of Jerusalem by the Babylonians, the successors to Assyria, and the exile to Babylon in the sixth century. But beginning at chapter 40, the portion known as "Second Isaiah," a new and hopeful note is sounded in the voice of a prophet writing at the time of the exile, predicting the fulfillment of God's promise to return the people from exile and restore them. The opening words of Second Isaiah are, "Comfort, comfort ye my people" (Isaiah 40:1 KJV). The later chapters of the book of Isaiah foretell of the coming of a just ruler, a Messiah who will suffer and triumph with the people. A number of passages from this later portion of Isaiah reappear in the New Testament, where the coming of Jesus is seen as a fulfillment of the prophecy and a continuation of the scriptural story of God's ultimate faithfulness to a vision of justice and universal peace.

One of the most joyful passages in the Bible, for me, is chapter 55 of the book of Isaiah, at the heart of the prophecy in Second Isaiah. What I find striking about this chapter of Isaiah is how vividly it renders God as the One who desires to heal, restore, and abundantly bless not only this redeemed people, but the whole of Creation. The abundance of the things that they need for life is interwoven seamlessly with the abundance that comes with knowing and following the will of a loving God—keeping the Covenant, as the Hebrew people understood it, and thereby living into the fullness of life that God intends for us all. I recommend spending some time with the whole of Isaiah, chapter 55. The chapter begins with God, speaking through the prophet, promising an abundance not only of food and drink, but of the divine presence in the people's lives:

Ho, everyone who thirsts,
come to the waters;
and you that have no money,
come, buy and eat!
Come, buy wine and milk
without money and without price.
Why do you spend your money for that which is not bread,
and your labor for that which does not satisfy?

Listen carefully to me, and eat what is good, and delight
yourselves in rich food.
Incline your ear, and come to me;
listen, so that you may live.
I will make with you an everlasting covenant,
my steadfast, sure love for David.

Isaiah 55:1-3

Imagine how this sounds to the descendants of people sent into exile forty years before. They are promised abundance of all the things they need, and also an ongoing relationship with the "steadfast, sure love" of their God. It is a glowing promise.

This passage also contains a question that invites our discernment, in our own time, about our relationship to the things that we have: "Why do you spend your money for that which is not bread, and your labor for that which does not satisfy?" In a consumerist society where the goal is always to have more, these questions have a resonance of their own. Even though money may be short, and even if we are carrying a lot of debt, we are constantly aware of opportunities to spend our money on all kinds of things, and sometimes convinced that we need much more than we actually do. We are also acutely aware in hard times of how much we need the basics of life, and we can grow fearful when money seems scarce. Paradoxical as it seems, stepping back and examining what we do with our money and our labor can actually be a practice of discernment, a way of noticing and embracing the abundance that God has given to us. It can also provide clues to who we are really made to be, and how we most deeply desire to live.

The Isaiah passage connects the abundance that comes from living by the Covenant with the assurance that God gives us what we need, both materially and spiritually. With this passage in mind, return to the words of Jesus in Matthew, and imagine a loving God asking you Jesus's question: "Where is your treasure? Where is your heart?" How might you respond?

Practice 2: Exploring Your Practices around Time, Money and Relationships

Spend some time with this grid, which invites you to explore your own practices and habits around time, money, and relationships. Fill in the grid without judgment or shame, just try to be as clear as you can about what your current practices tell you. What do you discover?

SPIRITUAL PRACTICES AROUND

WHAT PORTION OF YOUR TOTAL

MONEY

OBLIGATORY EXPENSES (rent, food, debt service, etc.)	DISCRETIONARY SPENDING (where you have a choice)

WHAT PORTION OF YOUR DAY OR

TIME

SCHEDULED/EXPECTED ACTIVITIES (work, family duties, etc.)	ACTIVITIES THAT FULLY ENGAGE YOUR ATTENTION (at work or elsewhere; you lose track of time)

HOW DO YOUR ANSWERS IN THE COLUMNS ABOVE

RELATIONSHIPS

TIME, MONEY, AND RELATIONSHIPS

EXPENSES DO YOU SPEND ON THE FOLLOWING?

TRUE-VALUE EXPENSES
(purchases that reflect your true values: you may "dig deep"
or save to make sure you can afford)

SHARING: GIVING TO OTHERS
(money set aside for God's work in the Church and world)

WEEK DO YOU SPEND ON THE FOLLOWING?

ACTIVITIES YOU MAKE TIME FOR
(even when you are very busy)

TIME FOR RELATIONSHIPS
(including communities and needs of others)

AFFECT IMPORTANT OR POTENTIAL RELATIONSHIPS IN YOUR LIFE?

A fundamental assumption throughout the biblical tradition is that even though we forget this often, everything we have is from God. The primary practice in relation to what we have is to give thanks for what we have—"counting your blessings." While this may seem unhelpful advice when someone suggests it in a time of loss, it can be an important way of staying mindful of what we have, especially when we feel anxious or fearful about money and resources. Nathan Dungan, creator of workshops on Financial Sanity, stresses the importance of looking at our attitudes toward money, thinking not only about how we spend what we have, but how we balance sharing, saving, and spending. Here are some questions he suggests you ask yourself, without judgment but in a spirit of exploration, as you begin to look more closely at your own practices and attitudes around money.[22]

- First, what is money for, in your life? Keep track of how you spend money for a week, or a month, and look at those amounts.

• What do you spend the most money on?

_____

_____

_____

_____

_____

_____

_____

_____

_____

_____

• What do you feel you don't have enough money for?

_____

_____

_____

_____

_____

_____

_____

_____

_____

_____

• Are you able to save any money regularly? How, and for what purpose? (Or, if you can't save now, what would you like to be able to
save for?)

_____

_____

_____

_____

_____

_____

_____

_____

_____

_____

• Do you make financial contributions to charities or church? How
often? How do you feel about these contributions?

_____

_____

_____

_____

_____

_____

_____

_____

_____

_____

- Do you find yourself worrying about money? What is the worry about?

  _____

  _____

  _____

  _____

  _____

  _____

  _____

  _____

  _____

  _____

- If someone gave you $100, what would you do with it?

  _____

  _____

  _____

  _____

  _____

  _____

  _____

  _____

  _____

  _____

Look at your answers. Talk them over with a friend or small group. What surprises you? What depresses you? What are you seeing about where money fits into your overall sense of meaning and purpose in life? As you look at your expenditures, think about how they match, or don't match, your values. How do you sort out wants, needs, and obligations? What does this tell you about your priorities?

As you sort this out, try bringing another lens to your stock-taking about money. Ask yourself, as you look at the figures you've written down, "Where is God in this, for me?" Return to the words of Second Isaiah, where God invites the people to pay attention to things they are buying that do not ultimately satisfy, and pay attention to what does:

> Why do you spend your money for that which is not bread,
> and your labor for that which does not satisfy?
> Listen carefully to me, and eat what is good,
> and delight yourselves in rich food.
> Incline your ear, and come to me;
> listen, so that you may live.
>
> Isaiah 55:2

This is poetry, not a game plan, but it contains the kind of promise that can shape our discernment around money. The prophet seems to be inviting people to see that God provides what we need. Do we believe this? This is a question that is at the heart of the spiritual practices around money that we find in scripture.

Practice 3: Tithing: A Traditional Practice around Money

The most striking, and perhaps most challenging for us in our current culture, is the practice of the tithe or the "first fruits" offering in ancient Israel. In this agricultural economy, the people are invited to offer back to God the firstborn of their flocks and the earliest fruits and vegetables of the harvest. Giving the first part of the harvest, rather than waiting to see what might be left over at the end, was a way of expressing, and even celebrating, the people's radical confidence that God would provide enough to meet their needs and would do so abundantly. In the book of Deuteronomy, the people are instructed to "set aside a tithe" (i.e., one-tenth) of all that their land produced, and bring it to a public place to create a feast for the community. What's striking about this is that the practice wasn't about funding a program of any kind, it was simply about setting aside the top ten percent and saying, "I don't need this. I have enough without it, by God's blessing. Let's use it to make a feast." Offering this off the top (rather than out of what is left over after other things were paid) reminded these ancient farmers that everything they had belonged to God. It expressed their faith that what was left over after that ten percent would be enough.

Read the description of the tithe and the feast in these verses:

> Set apart a tithe of all the yield of your seed that is brought in yearly from the field. In the presence of the LORD your God, in the place that he will choose as a dwelling for his name, you shall eat the tithe of your grain, your wine, and your oil, as well as the firstlings of your herd and flock, so that you may learn to fear the LORD your God always. But if, when the LORD your God has blessed you, the distance is so great that you are unable to transport it, because the place where the LORD your God will choose to set his name is too far away from you, then you may turn it into money. With the money secure in hand, go to the place that the LORD your God will choose; spend the money for whatever you wish—oxen, sheep, wine, strong drink, or whatever you desire. And you shall eat there in the presence of the LORD your God, you and your household rejoicing together.
>
> Deuteronomy 14:22–26

For the ancient Israelites, the bringing of tithes was meant to be a joyful practice, a way of feasting, giving thanks, and celebrating a connection with their God. What do you notice in this passage that seems familiar, or alien, or challenging? What works for you?

Deuteronomy specifies that the feasting was always to include the Levites, the priests who took care of the temple and presided over the people's religious life. Every third year, people were to set aside that tithe and store it for the Levites to live on since "they have no allotment or inheritance with you." The offerings set aside also supported widows and orphans, who did not have land and produce of their own. Through this practice of setting aside a portion for those who had none of their own, those whose land was fruitful made common cause with those outside the economic system. It was a practice that bound the community together and ensured that wealth was shared and everyone had enough.

Moreover, the Deuteronomy passage goes on to say that every seven years, the debts of anyone in the community would be forgiven. In Leviticus, we have the account of a Jubilee year every fifty years, when slaves were set free and debts forgiven. These practices created a level playing field among the Israelites, preventing anyone from growing hugely rich at the expense of their neighbor. These practices reminded everyone that the fruits of their labor ultimately came from God. God commands this practice, promising in return that "there will be no one in need among you." Whether it was always practiced faithfully is open to question, but this is the vision. The strongest condemnation from the prophets in Hebrew scriptures is addressed to those who had wealth and power yet failed to care for the poor among them.

The offering of first fruits, through the yearly tithe, together with the seven-year remission or the Jubilee, supported a whole system of values that reminded people of who they were in relationship to God, and expressed trust in God's goodness and in the support of the community of faith. Giving thanks was the core of these practices.

Paul endorses this practice of "setting aside a portion" for the benefit of the community and its leaders when he writes to the Corinthians about his plans to send envoys to them, urging them to take up a collection so that it will be ready, as a graceful gift, when those he is sending arrives. He is concerned primarily with the attitude of the givers in this circumstance, and his words suggest something also to us about our inner disposition in sharing what we have.

> Each of you must give as you have made up your mind, not reluctantly or under compulsion, for God loves a cheerful giver. And God is able to provide you with every blessing in abundance, so that by always having enough of everything, you may share abundantly in every good work.
>
> 2 Corinthians 9:7–8

Sadly, those words about God loving a cheerful giver have sometimes been used to guilt-trip people into giving what they don't want to give or are not really able to give. But the context is clear: giving, in the early Church, was thought of as coming out of abundance, and as expressing gratitude to God who has promised to provide abundantly for those he calls.

When the practice of tithing comes up among contemporary Christians, the conversation most often turns immediately to the *amount* of the tithe: "Why ten percent? Ten percent of what? Pre-tax or post-tax income? I don't know if I can afford that." These questions miss the point of the practice as it was followed in ancient Israel and as it has been followed in many Christian communities. The point of the practice of proportional giving is more radical even than the accounting questions that it most often raises. Ask yourself what would your family budget, what would your practices of spending, sharing, and saving look like, if you decided to take a fixed portion (one percent, three percent, five percent, ten percent—it doesn't matter) off the top, working with what remained as you made your financial plans? That money would go to something that reminds you of your dependence on God and your connection to a community of faith. It would be a concrete way of offering thanks for these gifts in your life.

If we understood this better, perhaps our churches would be places where people welcomed the chance to give as an expression of thanks, and our budgets would be built on trust that the people's offerings would be enough. And if they are not enough, this also presents opportunities for discernment about wants and needs in the life of the community. This may be scary for those of us who are also concerned with paying the bills that support a place for worship and educated clergy to lead us. But I wonder, what would it be like if churches presented the opportunities for giving as a spiritual practice that would help us in our discernment around our attitudes toward money?

Practice 4: Sabbath: A Traditional Practice around Time

We live with a widespread view that time is a limited commodity. There's not enough of it, every minute is filled, we have to "take time" for ourselves, and we need to "make time" for the things that are important to us. A whole variety of voices and institutions are competing for our time, trying to convince us that whatever activity they are offering is worth our time. This consumerist approach even affects our practice in churches, spurring efforts to market what we offer and attract new members by meeting their needs. Lost in all of this is an understanding of the Church as a place where we reconnect with the meaning and purpose of our lives, the dream of God for ourselves and for the world.

A return to some of the traditional spiritual practices around time can invite us into a place of astonishing, if countercultural, freedom. After all, time, like life itself, is a gift from a loving God who desires our thriving. Intentional spiritual practices centered around time can give us perspective about what our time is really for. Bonnie Thurston[23] makes this observation in her wonderful book, *The Spirituality of Time*:

> What we wish to spend our time on, what we desire to take time for, is not only defining of us, but is very likely God's call to us. This small quotation from Thomas Merton, which I clipped out of a missions newsletter long ago, focuses the issue powerfully: "If you want to identify me, ask me not where I live, or what I like to eat, or how I comb my hair, but ask me what I am living for, in detail, and ask me what I think is keeping me from living fully for the thing I want to live for." What do you live for? What do you want to live for? If the answers to these two questions are not the same, ask yourself: Why aren't they, and what can I do to harmonize my life.
>
> Thurston 2009, 40

The reality is that God has given us 24 hours every day. We have a number of choices about how we use that time, though often it doesn't feel as if we have a choice. As with our money, so with our time, it is true that "where our treasure is, there will our hearts be also." Take a moment, then, to look at your own attitudes toward time. Look over your calendar for the past week or two—enough to cover your "typical" schedule.

• How is your time divided up?

_____

_____

_____

_____

_____

_____

_____

- What do you spend the most time on?

_____

_____

_____

_____

_____

_____

_____

_____

_____

_____

- What do you feel you don't have enough time for?

_____

_____

_____

_____

_____

_____

_____

_____

_____

_____

_____

• What do you try to make time for, no matter how busy you are?

_____

_____

_____

_____

_____

_____

_____

_____

_____

_____

• Where were there interruptions or distractions disrupting how you thought you were going to be spending your time? How did you feel about those disruptions?

_____

_____

_____

_____

_____

_____

_____

_____

_____

_____

- What would you do with 24 hours of unscheduled time?

_____

_____

_____

_____

_____

_____

_____

_____

_____

_____

_____

_____

What do the answers to these questions tell you about what you are living for?

In the life of ancient Israel, the practice of Sabbath-keeping had the relationship to time that the practice of tithing had to money. It was a way to remind people that time is given in abundance, and to schedule into their lives a regular practice of rest. Just as God rested on the seventh day of Creation, so the people are called to rest and enjoy what God has made. The Sabbath (as Bonnie Thurston points out) is not to be seen as a set of prohibitions about what one must not do, but rather as a day of openness and rejoicing, when work and care are put aside so that we can enjoy our lives, in whatever way we choose to do so.

In our work-obsessed culture, the commandment to "remember the Sabbath, to keep it holy" is perhaps the most ignored commandment. If we are not working or being productive we may feel we are not important. And yet, in our obsession with work, we forget what life is for; we lose the ability to live in the moment. Bonnie Thurston warns against our obsession with "busy-ness," suggesting that it has deeper spiritual roots in an inability to trust that who we are is enough for a loving God, that we are "good enough."

> Nothing I "do" ultimately assures my value. My value as a human being is already secured by God as the source of my creation and by Jesus Christ as the source of my salvation. I may choose to engage in "good works"—benevolence, charity, whatever—as a grateful response to these gifts, but there is absolutely nothing I can do to earn them. The bottom line is I don't have to do anything; I just have to be, that is, to accept God's gift of life and respond by grateful living.
>
> Thurston 2009, 75–76

A practice of Sabbath-keeping, woven into the fabric of our lives, can help to restore the joy and fullness of life that God intends for us, and make us more able to embody that joy for others.

Look at your calendar and consider: Are there regular times that you set aside simply to enjoy the company of friends, relaxation, "down time"? Are there times set aside for prayer, reflection, exercise, walking in nature, or just watching a TV show or reading a book for fun? Bonnie Thurston suggests as a practice actually scheduling some time each week as Sabbath time—it needn't be a Sunday, though it may be—and set it aside as a time free of whatever you define as work. It may be an afternoon or an evening, a weekend day or two once a month, or a Sunday afternoon. Even when it is difficult to do, the exercise of trying to make time for Sabbath-keeping can help us to see where our hearts are and what we truly want in life. It can be a step toward discerning, in the midst of our busy-ness, the way that God desires to be with us, God's call to us in our lives. For a month or two, try to set aside four to eight hours a week as intentional, quality time with the God who loves you. Spend that time doing whatever makes you available to a sense of abundance in your life. Consider recording how you spend this time. What do you learn from this about yourself? What do you learn about who God wants to be for you?

All of this returns us, doesn't it, to the dream of God? It is God's desire that we might live and thrive, as God's people. The passages I have cited emphasize that the biblical view of money is one of abundance, not scarcity. The biblical world assumes that somehow or other, what we have been given will be enough. God's promise in Isaiah, Jesus's promise in the Sermon on the Mount, is that there will be enough, and more. To return to the promise of Second Isaiah, by appreciating God's abundance we participate in the joy of the whole Creation and, in doing this, we find ourselves changed, gradually learning to embrace and grow into the richness of God's will for us. Speaking through the prophet, God promises, in resonant poetry, to be faithful to the people as they celebrate the abundance of life:

> For you shall go out in joy,
> and be led back in peace;
> the mountains and the hills before you
> shall burst into song,
> and all the trees of the field shall clap their hands.
>
> Isaiah 55:12

Practice 5: Clarity Team Conversation around Time and Money

If it is your turn to be the focus person of your clarity team, you might invite your listeners to explore with you a challenge that has surfaced as you've looked at your priorities around time or money. Is there something that you are feeling called to change about your practice in these areas? What has surfaced for you as you worked through the time-money-relationship grid? If you are a listener, listen for where the Spirit may be moving for the focus person. If you are the convener, try to support the group's effort to probe what the challenge is here, and encourage people to avoid giving specific advice.

SESSION V

The Prayer Question

Prayer is responding to God, by thought and by deeds, with or without words.
(The Book of Common Prayer 856)

We turn to the prayer question after considering our practices around time. When I ask the question, "How do you pray?" people often answer with how they wish they could pray if only they had time, rather than pointing to particular practices that allow them to be open to the presence and mystery of the holy in our lives. The Book of Common Prayer defines prayer broadly as "responding to God, by thought and by deeds, with or without words," so the question about prayer really is, "How do you do that? How do respond to the holy in your daily life?"

I sometimes find that there is a lot of shame or embarrassment that emerges for people around this prayer question, but there is no "right" way to pray. The greatest prayer teachers frequently describe themselves as beginners at prayer. On the other hand, our Christian tradition does offer lots of guidance about the practices people have adopted as ways to respond to God's love and presence in our lives. The first step in thinking about prayer is to remember that its purpose is a deepening relationship. This means that even a desire to grow in prayer is already a gift of grace and a good step toward spiritual deepening.

A dear friend of mine taught me a lesson years ago about the purpose of prayer. It was my birthday, and both of us were at the seminary — she as a student in the Master of Divinity program, I as an adjunct faculty member.

The community in those days gathered every morning for Morning Prayer in the chapel, and after that the crowd flowed toward the next building where our mailboxes were. My friend approached me as we were leaving chapel. She had a lovely gift bag in her hand and she said, "It's your birthday! When can we get together for a few minutes today?" I was swept up in other demands and distractions before I had a chance to answer her, pulled aside by a student with a question, a colleague greeting me, milling around with the crowd. Finally, growing more and more impatient, my friend put herself in my path, holding up the gift bag, and said, "When can I have ten minutes of your time so I can give you this gift?"

When can I have some time so I can give you this gift? Imagine a God who is like that, who wants to give us gifts, rejoicing to watch us receive them. I have since thought of this incident as a parable for those times when I feel like I don't have time for any kind of dedicated or intentional prayer. It reminds me that the purpose of prayer is to show up, so that God can give us the gift of the fuller and deeper life that comes with an ongoing connection. For us as Christians, that connection somehow happens through our awareness of the living Christ in our lives, and by the Holy Spirit guiding us. We can look to the gospels for guidance about how to be available for these gifts.

Practice 1: Bible Study

A passage in the Gospel of Mark brings home both the desire and the challenges of spending time in prayer. Chapter 6 of Mark is jam-packed with action: the disciples are sent out to teach and preach, John the Baptist is killed by Herod, and Jesus and his disciples try to gather to be together, pray, and debrief. So, in verse 31, Jesus says to them, "'Come away to a deserted place all by yourselves and rest a while.' For many were coming and going, and they had no leisure even to eat." This coming away to spend time with Jesus is an image for what we seek in dedicated times of prayer. Elsewhere in the gospels it is at one of those times that Jesus teaches them the Lord's Prayer (Luke 11:1). But in this passage, no sooner have they gone away in their boat to a deserted place then they find that there is another crowd gathered to listen to Jesus teaching. There goes their time away.

This passage really spoke to me when I was in my early thirties, trying to build a career while also juggling real and valued family needs and demands. It seemed like there was no time anywhere to just "come away and rest" with God, even though it was also a time when that desire to grow in prayer was awakening in me. I ran across this passage from Mark one day when I was snatching a few minutes for scripture reflection, in preparation for a Bible study group at church. I had been saying to God, "I would really like to have a regular practice of prayer, but there doesn't ever seem to be time." And perhaps by the grace of the Holy Spirit, I encountered this passage in Mark where Jesus and the disciples, exhausted and seeking rest, find that, instead, they need to feed this crowd of 5,000 men, plus women and children, who have gathered to listen to his teaching. The disciples protest, "No way do we have enough bread to feed all these people!" And Jesus, instead of hearing "not enough," asks, "How many loaves have you?" The response "five, and two fishes" opens the way for the miracle of there being enough.

I heard the Spirit asking me, "You say you don't have enough time. How much time do you have? Do you have five minutes?" I thought I could find five minutes. And I started a practice of taking just five minutes in the morning for focused prayer, and letting that be enough. That has since grown into a valued morning time—for me, a time that has been the container for many different ways of prayer over the years. The time I've been able to allot for prayer has expanded as my desire has grown, so that indeed there has been enough time for prayer, but it started with this five-minute practice.

Practice 2: Showing Up for a Five-Minute Prayer

Something that may help you establish a five-minute prayer practice is the five-finger prayer, which is described here. First, take five deep breaths, to settle and focus. As you breathe in, welcome God's presence and love. As you breathe out, breathe out your distractions and worries. Then:

1. Hold out one finger, to begin the count, and say, "Oh God, you . . ." (form a sense or an image of the God who loves you, and quietly place yourself in that presence).
2. On the next finger say, "Thank you for . . ." and bring to mind anything you remember that you are grateful for today. Rest with this for five breaths.
3. On your third finger say, "I'm sorry for . . ." and bring to mind whatever you are regretting or feeling sorry for today. As you breathe in,

breathe in God's merciful love, and as you breathe out, breathe out what you are sorry for. Breathe this way four or five times.

4. On your fourth finger say, "Please help . . ." and bring to mind anyone you are praying for or anyone who has asked for prayers or seems to be in need. Hold their names in your mind as you breathe in God's love and breathe out all the hurt and pain and need. Take four or five deep, long breaths.

5. With all five fingers spread out, now say, "Please help me" and ask God for whatever you need today. Rest with this request for four or five deep breaths.

6. With both hands spread out and turned up to God (if this gesture is comfortable), end your prayer time by offering, very slowly, the Lord's Prayer.[24]

Note that this prayer practice can happen at any time during the day, but it's a good idea to choose a regular time and place: a prayer space in your home, or perhaps the moment when you turn on your computer in the morning, or some other routine moment that could open up into five minutes of intentional prayer.

Expanding the Five-Minute Prayer

My own experience with this was that I began with the five-minute prayer, but as time went on, I found that I looked forward to that brief time of prayer at the same time and the same place in the morning. The practice of just showing up was beginning to work on me, and as in the story of the feeding of the 5,000, God used what I had to offer to make more.

Here are some ways to pray that can grow out of the basic shape of practice of the five-minute prayer. See how this practice might work for you, depending on how much time you have to "show up" for prayer:

Do you have 10–25 minutes?
- Read all of Psalm 42, 63, or 103 to begin.
- Use the five-finger structure and slow down, lingering over each prayer. (Use your fingers to keep track of where you are.)
- End with the Lord's Prayer or, with a little extra time, use one of the short services collected in the Book of Common Prayer as "Daily Devotions for Individuals and Families" (The Book of Common Prayer 137–140)

Do you have 25–45 minutes?
- Expand the time you spend on each "finger" of your prayer. Breathe deeply and rest in the quiet as you pray, taking a full five minutes or more over each.
- In this amount of time, you can practice centering prayer. As described in session I, centering prayer creates a space in us where we can be "at home" with God and receive God's presence. Feel free to set a timer and spend, at first, five minutes in silence, then longer as you choose.
- There are other ways to become centered beyond sitting still. You might try the practice of "praying in color," where you use colored pencils or markers to focus your prayer, or color in a mandala, letting your mind settle on color and shape.

Do you have 30–60 minutes?
- Once you find yourself wanting to set aside more time, you can be creative about different prayer practices, remembering that the point is to show up for time with God. Holy reading, a regular practice of prayer with scripture, works well if you have a little more time to give to it.
- Or you may choose to pray in motion. Let a regular walk or run be your prayer. Take those first five minutes to use the five-finger prayer as a way to ground your desire to be with God. Let it set your intention as you begin to walk a labyrinth or begin a yoga practice.
- Or take the five-finger prayer on a walk. Walk a familiar path in nature or around your neighborhood, pausing at particular places to offer each step of the finger prayer, and letting the prayer deepen as you walk between parts of the prayer. I pause at the threshold to say, "O God, you . . ." I pause beneath the sycamore tree to say, "Thank you." I stop by the vacant lot to say, "I'm sorry for . . ." and so forth. After a while, the prayer and the walk will flow together.

Practice 3: A Practice for Paying Attention: Praying a Day of Life

If it is important, in our life of prayer, to have a practice that allows us to show up to receive God's gifts, it is equally important to develop some practices that enable us to check in with the Spirit along the way during our day. We are called to learn, gradually, in Paul's words, to "pray without ceasing" (1 Thessalonians 5:17). The exercise that follows invites you to journal about a day in your life and to practice noticing how God has been present, even if you didn't notice it at the time.

Give yourself about 30 minutes for this practice, which invites you to look back at a day that has passed. For starters, just pick a day from the previous week, or yesterday, or, if you're doing this in the evening, the day that has just passed. The value of this exercise is that it helps us to see, in retrospect, what we may not have seen as the day was passing — that a loving, guiding Spirit is present with us in every moment of our day if we take the time to notice. Indeed, even if we find that we're noticing an absence, that, too, is a turning toward the holy.

Begin this exercise, then, by choosing a day from the past week. If possible, choose the most routine, mundane, unmemorable day, or a day most typical of your daily routine, if there is such a day. Settle down into quiet, offer God thanks for the gift of that day, and then, without pausing over details, make a retrospective "What I did" list (got up, had breakfast, etc.), no more than eight or ten items, so that all the pieces of the day are listed. If you need to get out a calendar or phone to do this, go ahead, but then put it away!

What you come out with is a kind of personalized list of the "hours of the day." Most monastic communities, following the Benedictine tradition, establish hours of the day for work and prayer, for pause from work to turn to worship. The Anglican spirituality of the Book of Common Prayer is also Benedictine in its appointment of offices or prayer times at morning, midday, evening, and the close of day.

This exercise also has elements of the Ignatian practice of the Examen, a daily turning toward God to look back at a day of life. You can find more on the Examen here: https://www.ignatianspirituality.com/ignatian-prayer /the-examen/.

This is NOT meant to be an exercise in "how I could have done better" or an occasion for making resolutions or even for uncovering patterns or insights about how you deal with life. Try to put aside self-criticism, regrets, recriminations, even self-congratulation that may come to you as you recall your day. The point here is to look at God's *presence* in your day, not to look at yourself and how you did. This is not an evaluation but a prayer, so if you find yourself wandering into evaluation, try to turn to God quietly, simply, and offer back whatever is distracting you. Ask for the grace to attend quietly to God's presence. The Holy Spirit will teach you how to listen, if you desire to be taught. Express that desire in your prayer.

I
Morning

On this day the LORD has acted; we will rejoice and be glad in it. (Psalm 118:24)*

Spend a few minutes sitting quietly and recall before God the first part of the day you are remembering, from your first rising until about midday.

Ask the Spirit to guide you and imagine yourself back into one part of that morning—your rising, breakfast, the commute, your work, or someone you met. Stay with the first thing that you remember, and return to that time, in the presence of God. Sit with that memory in quiet, for a few minutes.

Write down a response to God's presence, or perhaps your desire for God's presence, in the moment you have been recalling.

_____

_____

_____

_____

_____

_____

_____

_____

_____

_____

_____

---

* In this exercise, quotations from the psalms are taken from the version in the Book of Common Prayer (BCP).

II
Midday

LORD, you have searched me out and known me;

you know my sitting down and my rising up; you discern my thoughts from afar.

You trace my journeys and my resting-places and are acquainted with all my ways.

Psalm 139:1–2

Moving now to the middle of your day, let the Holy Spirit guide your memory to one piece of that day—a meeting, a task, some work that you were given to do.

Remember this part of the day in the presence of God. You might try writing your recollection as a note to God, saying "you" to your Companion on the day's journey.

If you had a long afternoon, repeat this exercise with another part of the workday.

Write down an image or a few sentences to remind you of what you are noticing about these moments at the heart of your day.

_____

_____

_____

_____

_____

_____

_____

_____

_____

_____

III
Evening

Turn again to your rest, O my soul,

for the LORD has treated you well.

For you have rescued my life from death,

my eyes from tears, and my feet from stumbling.

I will walk in the presence of the LORD

in the land of the living.

Psalm 116:6–8

Now remember your home-coming—the commute, the transition from day to evening—whatever it was for you.

Remember, in God's presence, how you spent your evening.

Write down a few sentences recalling something you particularly remember about that evening – a person, an event, a detail of the evening's routine.

_____

_____

_____

_____

_____

_____

_____

_____

_____

_____

_____

_____

_____

_____

_____

_____

_____

_____

_____

_____

_____

_____

_____

_____

_____

_____

_____

_____

_____

_____

_____

_____

_____

_____

_____

_____

IV
Night

Behold now, bless the LORD, all you servants of the LORD,

you that stand by night in the house of the LORD.

Lift up your hands in the holy place and bless the LORD;

the LORD who made heaven and earth bless you out of Zion.

Psalm 134

Now, remember yourself going through your late evening routine, settling down to your night's rest.

Write down a prayer offering the day back to God, giving thanks for any insights about the day that the Spirit has led you to in this time of reflection.

_____

_____

_____

_____

_____

_____

_____

_____

_____

_____

_____

_____

_____

_____

V
Returning to the Present Moment

Look over your notes now and then put them aside and sit still, in the presence of God, remembering that the presence you have been discerning in the day that has passed is also with you, just as steadily and firmly, in this present moment. Wherever you are in your day now, stay for a few minutes in that presence, giving thanks in whatever way you can for God's love for you in the present moment.

Practice 4: From the Tradition: The Examen

The journaling exercise you've just experienced is a version of what St. Ignatius of Loyola called the Examen—a daily life review that is a bedrock of Jesuit spirituality. People usually practice the Examen in the evening, looking back at the day. There are many ways of guiding the process, but here is the one I have found easiest to remember: Begin by asking for the grace to see where God has been present in your life in the past day (or if, like me, you do the Examen in the morning, you look back at the day before). Then ask God, "Where did I meet you today? And where did I miss you?" and in memory go back through the day, much as you have done in the previous exercise, and pay attention to where God was present, and where you may have missed God's presence. Offer a quiet prayer of thanks for those moments of presence, and a gentle prayer of forgiveness for those missed moments.

The purpose of the Examen is to get in touch with God's continuing presence and love in our lives, even when we feel we have not deserved or noticed it. The Examen also helps us notice if there are patterns that are tending to move us away from God, and to push back against those patterns, asking for grace. There's also an app for that, "Reimagining the Examen," which offers different approaches to the Examen each day.

Practice 5: With Your Clarity Team

As the focus person in a clarity team, you might bring for exploration your questions about what ways of prayer seem to be drawing you at this time, or perhaps invite your listeners to help you explore something that seems troubling or "not working" in your life of prayer. As listeners, you would be paying attention to the movement of the Spirit, and learning where this person may be feeling drawn to a particular way of prayer. If you are the convener, try to encourage people away from specific advice, but do invite reflection at the end of what the group has been hearing. A lot can be learned by listening and then reflecting together.

A Reminder: What Prayer Is For

We pray in many ways—giving thanks, praising God, asking for what we need for ourselves and for others. But ultimately, the purpose of an ongoing prayer practice is to grow in our awareness of and relationship to the God who loves us and desires good for us and for all of Creation. It may involve dealing with hard things in ourselves and in our days, but a regular practice gradually opens us to deeper transformation and even peace. The fruits of prayer are hard to describe in words and they are different for everyone, but I leave you as this chapter closes, with this poem that attempts to give shape to my own experience of the gift of prayer at its best.

Reveling
Prayer, Teresa said, will finally be
A simple conversation between friends.
Beyond the drama and the wilderness
The dry places and the upwelling springs
At last, or intermittently, we settle
To daily conversation. That is all

And sometimes, as today, the conversation
Lapses. Nothing, really, now, to say
And even though the silence might appear
To be an invitation into some
Dramatic mystic moment, it is not
Exactly that. Rather, a simple reveling:
Contentment without content: resting in
The quiet being-here that long love brings.

SESSION VI

Imaging Vocation

As we move toward the end of these sessions, I invite you to pause and revisit the questions we began with. Your profile: What do you do? How do you present yourself to the world publicly? What is your passion? Your sense of purpose: Is it tied in with the dream of God? Who are your people? What practices help to keep you grounded in your life of faith? How do you pray? Vocation, I am suggesting, is what God is doing with your responses to all of these questions. Look again at the questions and sit with them for a few minutes, in quiet. What do you notice that may not have been obvious when you first engaged with these questions? Is there something emerging that you might pray with further or bring to a clarity team for further exploration?

Having looked closely at a number of approaches to discernment in these chapters, it will be helpful now to engage in a prayerful life review, to look at your own spiritual autobiography. There are many ways to do this, of course, because people's experiences of call vary. Kathleen Cahalan, in her book on vocation, offers three helpful images for ways that people tend to think about God's call in their lives: the acorn (which already contains all the DNA needed for the oak that will grow out of it); the journey, with stops along the way; and the "aha" moment, when everything seems to come clear all at once.[25] Related images, for me, have been the thread, the journey through fog, and the annunciation moment. These images take us beyond analysis and into imagination, and so for each of them, I want to offer some personal reflection and a piece of poetry to guide your reflection on God's call in your life.

Image 1: The Thread

For some people, a vocation emerges as the thing they have always known or felt drawn to, as long as they can remember; something that they feel they were "made for." William Stafford, in his poem "The Way It Is," invites us to contemplate a "thread" that goes through life, like a pattern in a tapestry.

> There's a thread you follow. It goes among
> Things that change. But it doesn't change.
> People wonder about what you are pursuing.
> You have to explain about the thread.
> But it is hard for others to see.
> While you hold it, you can't get lost.
> Tragedies happen, people get hurt
> or die; and you suffer and get old.
> Nothing you do can stop time's unfolding.
> You don't ever let go of the thread.[26]

Read this poem aloud, at least twice, paying attention to words or phrases that speak to you. What is the "thread" in the poem? What are we told about it? What qualities of the thread particularly strike you? What is that thread for you?

Now, your response here might be, "That's just the problem. I don't know what the thread is in my life. That's what I'm trying to figure out." But others may be able to point to patterns that have seemed meaningful.

Practice 1: Holding on to Your Thread

Here is an exercise to help you reflect on what that "thread" has looked like in your life.

- Find a piece of heavy twine, clothesline, or rug yarn. Or, if you prefer, a bead-stringing kit, with different colored beads. Go to your prayer space and center yourself. Then read the poem again.

- Invite the Holy Spirit to help you hold on to the thread, and then look back at your life so far, breaking it up into about five-year intervals. For each five-year span, tie a knot in your thread or add a bead to your string. Holding on to that knot or bead, reflect on what was important to you during those years of your life: people, places, work, play. Do this for each five-year span. When you get to where you are now, go back and just hold on to each knot or bead, taking three deep breaths for each, and remembering what that bead or knot reminds you of.
- You might want to put your string of beads in your pocket and take a walk, and as you do so, finger the beads or the knots, one by one, reflecting on God's presence (or absence) in that part of your life. What do you discover?
- Write down some reflections or draw in whatever art medium appeals to you or share what you have learned with your clarity team, inviting them to help you discern more fully what that thread is in your life, and how to hold on to it.

_____

_____

_____

_____

_____

_____

_____

_____

_____

_____

_____

_____

_____

_____

Image 2: The Journey through Fog

Another image that speaks to many is the image of the journey or pilgrimage. A classic text in the Orthodox tradition, *The Way of a Pilgrim*[27], tells the story of a monk who undertakes a journey, the destination unclear, in order to learn a practice of "praying without ceasing." As he walks, he fingers the prayer beads in his pocket and says the prayer that we know as the "Jesus Prayer:" "Lord Jesus Christ, Son of God, have mercy on me." What he finds is that this practice of being constantly at prayer makes him more alert and available to the people he meets along the way, more open to the transformation that God offers him at every step of the way. It is a story of practicing discernment. What stays with me about this story is the focus on the journey and not the destination. That is probably the hardest thing for us in our contemporary culture because we want to know "where this is going" or "what we're supposed to be doing."

The word *journey* evokes something more intentional than a trip. It is not just about getting to a destination by the most direct way possible. Rather, if you've been on a journey or a pilgrimage, you know that the events and obstacles we meet along the way teach us as much about ourselves as the ultimate arrival. A journey may have a map or compass to guide us, but there are always detours and discoveries.

When I do a vocational life review, I find that an image that has stayed with me came years ago when I was hiking with family in Olympic National Park, on the path up Mount Olympus. As we set out, we had a beautiful view of a valley studded with bright wildflowers and shadowed with dappled clouds, but as we went higher, the view both below and in front of us was obscured by a thick fog. All that we could see was the path under our feet, and the sounds around us were odd and muffled. My husband and kids ran ahead, eager to get to the summit, but I held back. I found myself intentionally taking the next step, and the next, hoping that eventually we'd come to a break in the clouds and another sunlit view.

They kept on hiking, intent on reaching the summit as quickly as possible, but I slowed down, letting my steps take me only as far ahead as I could see. And slowly, through the fog, I began to see what I might have missed — the colors of wildflowers along the side of the path, the traces of animals, the shapes of stones. I didn't know what we would find when we reached the summit, but I was grateful to see what I might have missed by going faster. This has become a go-to memory for me when in my journey of discernment I find myself "in a fog" — in a time of transition, or loss, or confusion. It is helpful to remember to pay attention to what is along the path. Doing so allows us to remember that when we follow Jesus, we don't always know where he is taking us.

The "journey through fog" image has come back to me at moments of transition in life. A poem that I wrote just as we were moving to a new home looks back at the journey through fog that I've just described. It invites a consent to that attitude of "unknowing" that is important to bring to all the moments of change and transition in our lives.

Unknowing
A few weeks from now we will move from here
To the new place we have chosen.
I will leave this patio, grey stone, red brick and green

Today I do not know what I will know soon
How much this house will sell for; when moving day will be
Who will live here next
I wonder how my morning solitary times will be
As we learn to live in our new place

Years ago, climbing Mount Olympus
We found ourselves surrounded
In thick fog. All that we could see
Was the path under our feet
And so we took the next step, and the next, hoping
That through the clouds, we'd come
To a sunlit view: white mountains, blue valleys
Wildflowers blooming purple pink.
But we could not know what we would see
Coming to that high place.

I lost my companions for a while, as the fog dropped.
They kept on striding, intent on the summit
But I slowed down

My steps took me only as far ahead as I could see.
Slowing, my mist-filled eyes began to see
What I might have missed, going faster:
By the side of the path, intense blue of mountain aster
Fire of devil's paintbrush
And tiny grey-green lichens, hanging on.

And so, I pause now, at this turning time
With mist-filled eyes
To gaze at where I am: grey stone, brick wall
The pink geranium where the hummingbirds have come
Chrysanthemums, burnt orange, on the patio wall
And the surrounding green that has been my home.
Not knowing what the move will make of me
When I come to our new place.

Young adult life is full of transitions and changes, and sometimes we get so occupied with controlling what comes next that we don't pay attention to where we are.

- Are you in a time of transition and uncertainty?

_____

_____

_____

_____

_____

_____

_____

_____

_____

- What would it be like to slow down and pay attention to the place where you are now, either physically or spiritually?

_____

_____

_____

_____

_____

_____

_____

_____

_____

_____

_____

_____

_____

_____

_____

_____

_____

_____

_____

_____

_____

_____

_____

_____

_____

- If you think of your life as a journey, what detours and obstacles have you encountered?

_____

_____

_____

_____

_____

_____

_____

_____

_____

_____

_____

_____

_____

_____

_____

_____

_____

_____

_____

_____

_____

_____

_____

_____

- Has your sense of the destination changed?

_____

_____

_____

_____

_____

_____

_____

_____

_____

_____

_____

_____

_____

_____

_____

_____

_____

_____

_____

_____

_____

_____

_____

• Do you sometimes wonder if you are just in a fog?

_____

_____

_____

_____

_____

_____

_____

_____

_____

_____

_____

_____

_____

_____

_____

_____

_____

_____

_____

_____

_____

_____

_____

_____

_____

_____

Practice 2: Prayerful Freewriting

Choose an image or phrase from the poem "Unknowing," write it down, say a short prayer for guidance, and then freewrite for four to five minutes (set a timer), just letting words flow without editing or analyzing. Where has the image taken you? What does your writing tell you about where you are right now on your journey? You might want to repeat this journaling exercise over several days. You may decide to take a word or phrase and use your colored pencils or watercolors to create an image that speaks to you of your own journey.

Where are you, right now, on your journey? What parts of the path ahead seem clear? Where is there fog? Share with a friend or with your clarity team, if you have one, what you have learned from this writing.

_____

_____

_____

_____

_____

_____

_____

_____

_____

_____

_____

_____

_____

_____

_____

_____

_____

Image 3: Annunciation Moments

A third image for vocation in our stories is what Cahalan calls the "aha" moment—the moment when a new path opens up in our lives that makes sense of everything that has gone before, and marks a moment of transformation, so that we recognize everything that follows it as part of a process of transformation. Sometimes we seize these moments, and sometimes we miss them, but they do come for some of us.

I have long associated the "aha" moments in my life with my favorite story of calling, the Annunciation to Mary in the Gospel of Luke (Luke 1:26–28). In the story, Mary is a young unmarried woman—probably a teenager, given the cultural norms of the time. She is alone in her home when an angel arrives and announces to her that she will have a child who will be the redeemer of God's people. There are many artistic depictions of this scene, and it is often cited in celebration of Mary's meekness and humility. But what strikes me in the story is Mary's clarity about what is happening, and her engagement with the angel. "How can this be?" she asks boldly, in response to the angel's message, and only after she receives a gentle explanation does she say, "Behold, I am God's servant, let it be to me according to your will." I have been particularly inspired by poets who point to Mary's courage and strength in this moment of consent, particularly the poem "Annunciation" by Denise Levertov. In that poem, she asks:

> Aren't there annunciations
> of one sort or another
> in most lives?[28]

A clear annunciation moment came for me in my late twenties, when I shifted my career track from a strong plan A to a plan B that I hadn't even realized was my true calling. Plan A was a smooth career track, from a prestigious Ph.D. in literature to a tenure-track teaching position. In the early years of that tenure-track job, I received a study grant that made it possible to take two years off from teaching and follow my husband to another city, where he had landed a high-powered postdoctoral position. The open time also made it seem possible to start our family, and so during my first year there, I worked diligently on what I thought would be my "tenure book," following the advice of wise female colleagues to "finish the book before you have the baby." I got pregnant on schedule and had worked out ways to combine at-home motherhood with the writing that my grant was funding. My husband was on board with plan A, which called for him to find a job back in the same city where we could both continue our careers in tenure-track positions, I in the humanities and he in medical science.

I remember vividly the setting of my annunciation moment. I was in the kitchen of our messy duplex apartment, with its apricot walls and pressboard paneling. As usual, the table was sticky and there were dishes in the sink. There was a wash load running in the portable washing machine next to the kitchen sink. My two-year-old, in his highchair, was rubbing his hands in his Cheerios. It was late winter. My husband was out of town, interviewing for the faculty position that was the lynchpin of plan A, a plan that also would take us back to the church and community that had nurtured us in the early years of our marriage. It was around suppertime, and the phone rang. It was my husband, announcing, "I've got the job! We're all set. We can do it. We come back in the fall. You go back to your job. It's all set!"

In that moment I knew, suddenly, that I did not want to go back to my tenure-track job. I did not want the plan A that had always been the assumed path of our life. The place where I was just at that moment— that messy kitchen and sticky table, with this garrulous toddler in his highchair—was the place where I wanted to be, where I felt called to be. I did not realize until that moment that this was where I most deeply belonged. A few months later I stepped off the tenure track and turned from the standard academic path to a path whose destination I could not see, one that took us to a new community and a transformed direction, one that I've been figuring out, step by step, ever since.

When I remember that moment, the room comes into focus, the phone call breaking into that January evening routine, perhaps as the angel's presence did to Mary. What I felt was clarity, a deep "yes" to a question that had not been articulated, but that was calling out something in me. A new pathway opened for me that evening, and it is the path I have been on ever since. All I knew at the time was that this was right. It was what I really wanted, and in some sense, what the universe wanted of us at that moment. It was an experience, for me, of annunciation, or call. What I would describe later on as "the deep truth/I'm a mom" (see session I) was revealed to me in that moment. And ever since then, that choice has shaped my career path—teaching and writing in a variety of contexts, raising a family, and never being quite able to explain to people my scattered but ultimately satisfying resume.

Practice 3: Meditation on Your Annunciation

Read over the story of the Annunciation to Mary in Luke, using the Ignatian method of imaginative prayer described in session II. Have there been moments of "annunciation" in your life — times when everything came clear for a moment and you could say "yes"? Once you remember your annunciation moment, go back to it in your imagination, remembering with as much detail as you can what it was like for you. Where were you? What were the sights, smells, and sounds? How did you respond to your annunciation? How does that memory connect to the moment you find yourself in now?

Write down what you discover. You might choose to share with a friend or your clarity team what this meditation tells you about your own experience of annunciation.

_____

_____

_____

_____

_____

_____

_____

_____

_____

_____

_____

_____

_____

SESSION VII

Discipline, Discipleship, Discernment

Do not be conformed to this world, but be transformed by the renewing of your minds, so that you may discern what is the will of God.

Romans 12:2

I am with you always, to the end of the age.

Matthew 28:20

I remember a conversation with a beloved colleague and mentor, a man who had been a monk earlier in his life but later left the order, married, and became a leader and teacher in the church, with all the administrative responsibilities that involves. He lost his beloved wife suddenly, and plunged into a time of deep grief, bordering on clinical depression. When I asked him how he was doing, he said, "I would be lost without my discipline."

"I would be lost without my discipline." That word *discipline* stuck with me because it has the same root as *disciple*. A disciple is someone who is taught and guided by a master or spiritual teacher, and who shapes their own life around those teachings. And this friend was a disciple for sure; someone who had developed a lifelong habit of prayer, study, and service. In this time of grief, his daily prayer practice was exceedingly dry for him, but the discipline itself, he said, saved him from despair. "I would be lost without my discipline." The metaphor was of orientation: his discipline, his daily practice and rule of life, kept him oriented, the way a compass keeps explorers oriented and enables them to find their way. His discipline helped him to keep his orientation toward God, even when he wasn't feeling much at prayer at all.

For some of us, discipline is associated with shame or punishment, though its basic meaning connects more with faithfulness. A classic work on spiritual practices by Richard Foster is called *A Celebration of Discipline*[29] and invites us to think of a discipline as a practice. A spiritual discipline or practice is something we do regularly, whether we want to or not, and whether it is satisfying or not, to make room in our lives for the God who loves us and desires to shape our lives into lives that will help to shape and serve God's own dream for the world God loves. The poet W.H. Auden writes of practicing the "scales of rejoicing."[30] We may not always be good at it, but it's something we do in order to grow more able, more available, for whatever vocation is active in our lives.

We have explored a number of practices or spiritual disciplines that can help us grow in our ability, willingness, even eagerness to follow Jesus. As we grow into a faithful life, a life of discipleship, one of the important tools to develop is a *rule of life*. Esther de Waal[31] tells us that in the monastic rule observed in Benedictine communities, there are three basic building blocks. The first is *stability*: the commitment to dwell in a particular community, observing its routines and joining in its work, observing a particular set of prayer-practices a regular way, showing up daily to the mode of life chosen. Those of us living in the ordinary, secular world live into this sense of stability by having a regular time and place where we show up for prayer, a regular practice of worship, places of prayer and community that we return to, whatever is going on in the world around us. Showing up regularly for some kind of worship in community is the practice that supports this aspect of stability.

The second building block in this monastic tradition is *obedience*, which de Waal reminds us has its roots in the same Latin word as *listening*. The rule of obedience is what de Waal elsewhere calls the "spiritual discipline of attentiveness."[32] Listening and paying attention are the foundations of the practices of discernment this series has been inviting. Paying attention to the ways that we encounter God over the course of our day and our lives is a way of committing to listening as an ongoing practice. All of the tools for discernment suggested in this study can be ways of living into a way of obedience, of faithful listening or attending to God in our lives.

The third building block for Benedictines is *conversion*, an openness to transformation. The word *conversion* is sometimes associated in our minds with a radical change, a turning from one belief system or way of life to another that happens once and for all. It may conjure up for some of us the idea of a single moment, an altar call or a sudden and dramatic shift or revelation that sets us on some new religious path. But the Benedictine understanding, which is also foundational to our Anglican/ Episcopalian way, sees conversion as an ongoing process, a daily opening to God's will that recognizes our need to be on a constant journey of change, renewal, and transformation, open to the Spirit's leading. This leads to the purpose of a rule of life—to keep us open to discernment.

Practice 1: Bible Study

A good text for exploring this openness to transformation is Romans 11:33–12:2, where Paul reminds us how much bigger God is than anything we can grasp or define, and then invites us boldly to engage with that God, opening ourselves to transformation. Sit with this passage and pay attention to the words or phrases that shimmer for you here.

> I appeal to you therefore, brothers and sisters, by the mercies of God, to present your bodies as a living sacrifice, holy and acceptable to God, which is your spiritual worship. Do not be conformed to this world, but be transformed by the renewing of your minds, so that you may discern what is the will of God—what is good and acceptable and perfect.
>
> Romans 12:1–2

"Do not be conformed to this world, but be transformed by the renewing of your mind, so that you may discern." Openness to transformation— what Ignatius of Loyola calls freedom—is necessary for genuine, faithful discernment. Practices that can help with this renewing of the mind include regular study and reading. Sabbath rest and tithing, discussed in a previous chapter, can also be parts of a rule of life that open us to transformation.

Practice 2: Shaping a Rule of Life

A good image for a rule of life is a compass, the instrument that keeps us oriented toward the direction we need to go in. A compass doesn't judge us or shame us, it simply shows us the way. And when we get off course, we can consult the compass to find the way back. Like a compass, a rule of life serves to orient us. In order to be helpful, it needs to be simple, with just a few regular practices that we can identify and return to. I usually advise people to shape a rule of life that includes the following:

1. A way of showing up daily for prayer—at some specified time and place, even for a short time. The five-finger prayer discussed in session V can help provide a framework for this.
2. A way of paying attention—noticing as we go through the day those moments when we are most aware of God's presence, or sometimes of God's seeming absence, and our own longing in our lives.
3. A way of staying open to discernment, for ongoing change. A good rule of life includes some practices that help us remain increasingly open to the transformation that God always invites, from where we are to who we are becoming, fishermen to "fishers-of-men." Study and reading, manual work that allows you to learn more about nature and the world, spending time with people different from yourself and outside your immediate orbit, participating in work you feel called to, engaging in work that serves what you are seeing as the dream of God in your context—all of these invite the Holy Spirit into our lives and open us to change.

For me, as for many, the COVID-19 pandemic of 2020–2021 brought some fresh insight into the purpose of a rule of life. My own rule of life includes regular worship and Eucharist, time set aside for prayer and scripture study each morning, and ongoing volunteer work with people who are dealing with homelessness and poverty. Tithing (giving away a portion of what we've been given) and Sabbath time—rest from work—have also belonged to my personal rule. To this I added more recently an openness to conversation around issues of class and racism, from where I live as a white person in American society, with intercessory prayer tied to reading and following the news.

But the news part became outsized and even overwhelming as we dealt with the pandemic, protests against racial violence, and the 2020 election, and I recognized how much of my rule of life, as well as my vocation as a teacher, has relied on gathering in person with people and listening to a variety of voices both within and beyond my family and community of faith. Health issues in my family kept us pretty much self-quarantined for most of the pandemic, so I was finding new ways to carry on this rule via Zoom, but one thing that really couldn't happen was a Sabbath practice of going away for a quiet retreat at least once, and preferably twice, a year. That, and a long stretch without Eucharist, had the effect at first of just leaving me frustrated, but as time went on, I came to see that my longing for these practices was actually a way of deepening my connection with God, even though it felt like dryness. I *missed* parts of my rule of life when I couldn't observe them as I had wanted to, for reasons beyond my control. Just being in touch with that desire for God was strengthening, even when it was frustrating. It helped to reorient me, to show me that I was still on the path.

During the pandemic we were given a lot of good advice about self-care — be sure to be in touch with people, get out and walk in nature, go easy on yourself, don't overdo the Zoom, take a Sabbath from immersion in news and Twitter — and all this was good for general sanity. But the rule of life has a different purpose from self-care. It wasn't mainly to relieve stress or help me feel better; it was to keep me oriented toward God and open to discernment about where the healing and reconciling power of God might be active, even in a challenging time. That is why the image of a compass works for me, as an image for a rule of life. It is the set of practices that keep us oriented toward the holy in our lives. Even when it is difficult or impossible to observe a whole rule, our commitment to a rule provides a way to keep us oriented toward discipleship, and helps us to live in hope, even in challenging situations.

Questions for Reflection

- What aspects of your own current life help you to be open to transformation?

  _____

  _____

  _____

  _____

  _____

  _____

  _____

- How do you "show up" for God in a regular way?

_____

_____

_____

_____

_____

_____

_____

_____

_____

_____

- What practices help you "pay attention" to the ongoing presence of God in your life?

_____

_____

_____

_____

_____

_____

_____

_____

_____

_____

_____

- What practices keep you open to transformation, willing to be changed in ways that will help you to live more faithfully and joyfully, participating in God's dream of reconciliation and healing for the world?

_____

_____

_____

_____

_____

_____

_____

_____

_____

_____

_____

Practice 3: Guided Meditation on the Disciples' Commissioning

Remember that in the story of the fishermen in the Gospels of Matthew and Mark, Jesus invited the disciples, "Follow me, and I will [make you to become] fishermen for people?" He met them where they were and invited them to a transformed version of their present identity, life, and work. In the last paragraph of Matthew's gospel the risen Christ has been with the disciples and now he is leaving his work to them.

Now the eleven disciples went to Galilee, to the mountain to which Jesus had directed them. When they saw him, they worshiped him; but some doubted. And Jesus came and said to them, "All authority in heaven and on earth has been given to me. Go therefore and make disciples of all nations, baptizing them in the name of the Father and of the Son and of the Holy Spirit, and teaching them to obey everything that I have commanded you. And remember, I am with you always, to the end of the age."

Matthew 28:16–20

He tells them, "Go, and make disciples of all nations." The Greek word for "make disciples" also could be translated as "teach." He is sending them out beyond their traditional boundaries, to "all nations," to share what they have learned from following him.

This instruction to "make disciples" might strike some of us the way "fishers-of-men" did. What exactly does it look like to make disciples when we're not even sure how to be disciples ourselves? Brian McLaren has suggested that our fundamental purpose as Christians is "to be and to make disciples of Jesus, for the good of the world."[33] This meshes with Verna Dozier's understanding of the people of God as those who help to realize the "dream of God," beginning where we are.

Some branches of Christianity emphasize making disciples as a matter of persuading people to make a statement of faith, to accept Jesus as Lord and Savior in order to be saved. Our tradition in the Episcopal Church is also grounded in Jesus, but it tends toward an understanding of Christian discipleship that is directed, not so much toward individual salvation, as toward God's love for the world, and our participation in carrying that love.

At every baptism, in the ritual of renewing our baptismal covenant, we actually commit to a rule of life that begins with our own practices and turns us out toward the world that God loves. We promise to "continue in the apostles' teaching and fellowship, the breaking of bread and the prayers" and to "persevere in resisting evil," to be willing to repent and return to God when we fall into sin; that is, to "show up" and to "pay attention," and to be open to conversion. This openness to conversion also turns us outward toward the world. We promise to "seek and serve Christ in all people," loving our neighbor as ourselves and to "strive for justice and peace among all people and respect the dignity of every human being." All of these promises serve as our response to Jesus's commissioning, to proclaim, by word and example, the "good news of God in Christ." The baptismal promises remind us of what it means to live as disciples of Jesus and to proclaim the good news "by word and example." As we live into a rule of life that includes openness to discernment, we begin to see how we are called, individually and as communities, to serve God's dream for humanity, relying on the One we follow, in love. The prayers and the practices are the foundations of our discipleship (The Book of Common Prayer 304–305).

"Remember, I am with you always, to the end of the age," says Jesus, in his last words to the disciples before his ascension. The "you" here is plural, speaking to all disciples, but of course, each of them would have heard it as a personal message.

How do you experience this promise? What is your response?

_____

_____

_____

_____

_____

_____

_____

_____

Now, look at how the story is expanded in the Gospel of Luke:

Then he said to them, "These are my words that I spoke to you while I was still with you—that everything written about me in the law of Moses, the prophets, and the psalms must be fulfilled." Then he opened their minds to understand the scriptures, and he said to them, "Thus it is written, that the Messiah is to suffer and to rise from the dead on the third day, and that repentance and forgiveness of sins is to be proclaimed in his name to all nations, beginning from Jerusalem. You are witnesses of these things. And see, I am sending upon you what my Father promised; so stay here in the city until you have been clothed with power from on high."

Luke 24:44–49

Jesus promises to send the Holy Spirit ("what my Father has promised") to guide and help the disciples. This is fulfilled later, in Acts 1 and the story of Pentecost, but here he reminds them that they are "witnesses" to all that has happened in their life with him. The invitation is to remember where we have witnessed the action of the Holy Spirit in our lives, where we have been able to see something about what it might mean to continue as disciples of Jesus.

Here's a meditation that invites you to look at your own story within the context of this strange story of sending that concludes the gospels and opens the book of Acts. You can see yet another version in Acts 1.

Take a few deep breaths and invite the Holy Spirit to direct your memory and thoughts. Have colored pencils or pens handy as you reflect on some of the following prompts.

Step 1: Background

In Luke, the risen Jesus tells his disciples, in a scene of tremendous joy, that "repentance and forgiveness of sins" are to be preached to "all nations." The good news is that God loves and wants to restore humankind, to include all nations in the promise made to Abraham. The disciples are to be "witnesses"—bearing testimony to what THEY have experienced. Their charge is to carry on Jesus's ministry. There is work to be done, and he is going to do it through them. In Matthew, Jesus tells his disciples, "I am with you always, to the end of the age." In Luke/Acts he promises to send the Holy Spirit to them. Though the stories are about his parting from them, they are also, paradoxically, about the ongoing presence of the risen Jesus with the Church, continuing to call us to discipleship.

Each of us has also experienced, in some way, this ongoing presence of Jesus in our lives, though we may not name it in this way. I invite you to reflect now on some of the "God moments" in your life to help you get a sense of what you are called to "bear witness" to, as the particular person that you are.

Step 2: Prayer Prompts for Journaling

I invite you then to a time of prayer and guided journaling. Begin by breathing in and out, and quietly repeat Jesus's words: "Remember, I am with you always, to the end of the age."

The following questions invite you to an experience of remembering or "witness." Remember when you have had some passing sense of the holy in your life—in nature, in people, awareness of something "other" breaking in quietly or dramatically into your life. It may have been a time of great joy, or sorrow, or confusion. Rest with each of these questions and pay attention to what comes up for you.

- What is your earliest recollection of God/Jesus/Spirit alive in the world? Stay with this, remember it. Write a note to yourself about it or simply breathe a prayer of thanks.

_____

_____

_____

_____

_____

_____

_____

_____

_____

_____

_____

_____

_____

_____

_____

_____

_____

_____

_____

_____

_____

- Think of a "God moment" in elementary school. Stay with it, remember it. Write a note to yourself about it or draw a picture to remind you.

_____

_____

_____

_____

_____

_____

_____

_____

_____

_____

_____

_____

_____

_____

_____

_____

_____

_____

_____

_____

- How about junior high or middle school years? Where or when were you very aware either of presence or absence of the holy in your life? When did you have a chance to serve someone else in a way that gave you joy, and perhaps a clue to a path of discipleship?

_____

_____

_____

_____

_____

_____

_____

_____

_____

_____

_____

_____

_____

_____

_____

_____

_____

_____

_____

_____

_____

_____

- Think about high school. If more than one time comes to mind, write a note to yourself about it.

_____

_____

_____

_____

_____

_____

_____

_____

_____

_____

_____

_____

_____

_____

_____

_____

_____

_____

_____

_____

_____

- Now go, in your memory and imagination, to your years since high school. What has been an important shift in your life since then, in education, or work, or relationships? Write a note to yourself about it or draw something to remind yourself. Sit quietly for five breaths with what you have written down. What else do you remember? Repeat the process again.

_____

_____

_____

_____

_____

_____

_____

_____

_____

_____

_____

_____

_____

_____

_____

_____

_____

_____

_____

_____

- What about recently? When have you been aware of a sense of presence, mystery, meaning in your life in the last few months?

_____

_____

_____

_____

_____

_____

_____

_____

_____

_____

_____

_____

_____

_____

_____

_____

_____

_____

_____

_____

_____

- Now, remember this promise of Jesus: "You are a witness..." "I am with you always, to the close of the age." Where can you hear this promise resonating in the moments of your life you are remembering?

_____

_____

_____

_____

_____

_____

_____

_____

_____

_____

_____

_____

_____

_____

_____

_____

_____

_____

_____

_____

- Sit with what has come to you in this time of meditation and journaling, and take about five minutes to freewrite. You may want to begin by asking the Holy One "What's next?" in your life.

_____

_____

_____

_____

_____

_____

_____

_____

_____

_____

_____

_____

_____

_____

_____

_____

_____

_____

_____

Close your time of meditation with this prayer of St. Teresa of Avila:

Christ has no body now on earth but yours;
Yours are the only hands with which he can do his work,
Yours are the only feet with which he can go about the world,
Yours are the only eyes through which his compassion can shine forth
upon a troubled world.
Christ has no body now on earth but yours.

Discernment and Discipleship: The Ongoing Conversation

"Go make disciples," the risen Christ tells his followers the last time they
see him on earth. Teach people that there is a better way. Be messen-
gers of that way. Form communities that work together in love—beyond
tribe, party, sect—where God's dream is central and we are committed
to discerning and participating in it. This is the calling to discipleship
and, let's face it, it is really hard to keep track of. It was in Jesus's time,
and it is now. Think about the world in the gospel story. The first disciples, fishermen, were changed by their experience of following Jesus; of
staying with, abiding with him; of healing and feeding people alongside
him; of preaching a love that both suffers and transforms. To be disciples,
for them, was to have a purpose, centered in that relationship with Jesus,
but also oriented toward teaching an oppressed and silenced people to
claim their core of faith, to believe that healing is possible. Remember[34]
how Jesus proclaims his mission, preaching in Nazareth at the beginning
of his ministry and quoting the prophet:

The Spirit of the LORD is upon me,
because he has anointed me
to bring good news to the poor.
He has sent me to proclaim release to the captives
and recovery of sight to the blind,
to let the oppressed go free,
to proclaim the year of the LORD's favor.

Luke 4:18–19

Following Jesus during his lifetime, the disciples were learning to
participate with him in serving this vision. Following the risen Christ

in our time, and empowered by the Holy Spirit, disciples of Jesus are called to serve the same vision, however elusive it may seem. To be a disciple of Jesus is to participate in a vision for human thriving that transcends whatever allegiances — to a particular historical time, class, tribe, culture — demand of us. It is to be part of what Bishop Michael Curry calls the "Jesus Movement,"[35] a movement that is founded by the risen Christ himself in this scene at the end of the gospel stories in Matthew and Luke. Verna Dozier reminds us of the biblical distinction between the "kingdoms of this world" and the kingdom, or reign, of God. Archbishop Desmond Tutu puts this vision in more modern terms in his book, *God Has a Dream*.

> "I have a dream," God says. "Please help me to realize it. It is a dream of a world whose ugliness and squalor and poverty, its war and hostility, its greed and harsh competitiveness, its alienation and disharmony are changed into their glorious counterparts, when there will be more laughter, joy, and peace, where there will be justice and goodness and compassion and love and caring and sharing. I have a dream that swords will be beaten into plowshares and spears into pruning hooks, that my children will know that they are members of one family, the human family, God's family, my family."
>
> Tutu 2005, 19–20

"I came that they may have life, and have it abundantly" Jesus says (John 10:10). This is the vision he commissions his disciples to serve, and this is the vision we are still called and empowered to serve. In the Ascension story, Jesus declares that he has already established his reign, and the disciples' role is to announce and serve that reign, which is often hidden and repressed in the midst of human abuse and suffering. This is why discernment is the practice at the heart of discipleship. Disciples need to cultivate ways to look, attend, and really see the places, relationships, and situations where the holy work of healing and reconciliation has begun and is continuing. The call to discipleship is, thus, always a call to ongoing discernment, challenging us to see and proclaim where God's transforming work is happening in the world, to participate in that work, and to amplify it, knowing that it can be costly, and that we may not always see its fulfillment.

Remember: that word *disciple* is translated from a Greek word that comes from the verb "to learn." A disciple is always a learner, and the learning is lifelong. The core relationship of the disciples to Jesus is that he is their teacher. When Mary Magdalene meets the risen Christ on the first Easter, she at first fails to discern who he actually is, mistaking him for the gardener. But when he calls her by name, her response recognizes that core relationship: *Rabboni* – "teacher."

We are still called to be disciples of the living Christ, learning from him as we meet him in the situations and relationships of our lives.

What's Next? Some Suggestions and a Poem

As you come to the end of this series, I hope you will begin to see that discernment is an ongoing process, always in conversation with our call to discipleship, and always shaping us to go deeper in a way that also helps to pull together some of what was learned from this series of workshops. This may be done in many ways. You may want to consider continuing the clarity team practice, meeting regularly with a trusted group. Take turns, at different sessions, being the focus person, beginning with this question or one like it: "Here's what I'm seeing/wondering/asking about my piece of God's work in the world. Can you help me, in this prayerful process, to clarify what I'm seeing?" From this, you may well find that more specific questions and insights emerge about your vocation to discipleship.

I also encourage you to find your own words for the good news that you are discovering as you explore the process of discernment and discipleship. Imagine someone asking you a question about your faith. How might you respond? I leave you with a poem that came out of me in response to a question from a friend. Think about hard questions that someone might ask you and try the process of breathing and then freewriting that you have been engaging in throughout this study. See what comes. Share it with a friend or a group.

Here's my own poem. As its title suggests, it is a provisional answer to a hard question. What in this poem might speak to you?

Stumbling Credo
Lines written in response to a friend who asked me, "What does the Crucifixion mean, anyway?

The world is broken: there's no doubt
about that part. People are cruel and violent
and the ones who are in power
religious or imperial, they know
their power rests on privilege and fear.

And yet there is, beneath it all, a love that is for all
that calls us home to ancient faithfulness
and gives the dispossessed a voice, a place, a grounded life.
It seems such love cannot prevail, when those who rule
and profit from the broken world, create a reign of fear.

But when that love, which has a human face
cannot endure to see how people harm each other
he comes to be among us, lives a human life, and shares the fate
of those the most oppressed, and says:
You are all God's people: rich and poor, in and out.
You are all so greatly beloved!

So stop this now. Repent, he says to all.
Change your way of life. Love one another, and resist
the rule of those who lord it over others. Turn from fear.

Such love, it seems, cannot survive
in such a broken world.
So his own leaders work together with
the rulers of the age. Call him a traitor,
kill and torture him,
And crucify: the punishment of rebels.

They can crucify the man, but they cannot kill
the love he bears and is,

nor can anything blot out this love.
The suffering is real. The love persists, And so
He rises from the dead, to say
Look: you cannot kill it.
He comes back to his closest friends and says again
I am the way. Follow me.
The work I brought has already begun. Let us continue.
There is still a Way.

There is still a Way, and it involves following Jesus, and growing in our clarity and availability as disciples, to carry out what our catechism calls "Christ's work of reconciliation in the world" (The Book of Common Prayer 855). As we continue on this path of discipleship, and grow into a rule of life, a guiding question might be, "What if it's all true?"

What if it's all true? What if the ground and source of our being, our life, our connections with one another and the earth, is real and alive, though beyond our ability to name it? What if this reality is best described and apprehended in personal terms, through our human images of love—mother-love, father-love, the love of devoted friends, the love of an artist or a gardener for what they have made or nurtured, the love that desires, above all things, the well-being of the beloved? What if it's all true? What if the heart of reality is that love?

And what if it's true, as we Christians claim (set our hearts to, as the word "credo" implies) that this love became human, took on fully our experience of bodily life, limiting itself (himself/herself—for this is a personal reality) to a person in history, with parents, friends, enemies, a culture, a community? What if Jesus *is* the Word made flesh, "incarnate" as we say. A mystery beyond our understanding, perhaps, but what if it's true? What if, fully human, he experienced what it is to be loved and cared for, and to be oppressed, rejected, betrayed, killed? And what if the witness of all those early disciples is true—that death could not contain him? That the life Jesus lived and brought and called us to is actually eternal life, and has already begun, even in a broken world?

And what if it's true that that life and love cannot be killed? What if, in the life of Jesus, in companionship with him, we can relearn that love at the heart of Creation, and embody it in our lives here and now? What if he really does live on in the gathered worshipping community (*ekklesia*) that we call the Church? It seems so unlikely, and yet what if, through all our divisions, abuses, human distortions, and misunderstandings of the good news, his life still lives in us? What if we are held, despite it all, in something that could be called the "divine love"?

And what if it is still possible to somehow be, in this world, that risen body of the Holy One, through our life together, through our relationships, through the choices we make for ourselves and for others? And what if there is power available to us, beyond what we can find within ourselves, to become what we were made to be—whole, and just and loving, bearers of the divine love? What if there is a Holy Spirit, working through us, that really can transform and change? What if the whole thing is a whole lot bigger than we thought? What if it's all true?

The path of discipleship, grounded in love and community, helps us to live into this hope that it's somehow all true, even if we don't always get it exactly right. With this hope we can continue on the path of a faithful life of discipleship, always growing and deepening as we come to know ourselves and our callings more clearly. The practice of discernment helps keep us on that path, going ever deeper into ourselves and the ways that God reaches out to us, and learning to be ever more attentive to the particular ways that we are called and empowered to serve the world that God loves. I hope that the tools of discernment offered in this book will continue to provide you with strength for this exciting journey.

Appendix: Scripture Passages on the Call of God

Use any of these passages for the methods of meditation with scripture suggested in this book

Scripture on God's Call:

The call of Abram: Genesis 12:1-3

Moses & Burning Bush: Exodus 3:1-14

The call of Samuel: 1 Samuel 3:1-11

Elijah (the still, small voice) 1 Kings 19:8-13

Gideon: Judges 6:36-40

The call of Isaiah: Isaiah 6:1-8 (9-13)

The call of Jeremiah: Jeremiah 1:1-9 (10-19)

The Annunciation to Mary: Luke 1:26-38

The call of the fishermen: Matthew 4:18-21, Mark 1:16-20

Luke 5:1-11(Simon Peter); (post resurrection): John 21:1-19

Jesus' call to John's disciples (Andrew, Peter, Philip, Nathanael): John 1:35-51 (including "Come and see" John 1:39)

The call of Matthew/Levi the tax collector: Matt 9:9(10-13); Mark 2:13-14 (15-17); Luke 5:27-28 (29-32) (followed by dinner and "I have come to call not the righteous but sinners, in all 3 synoptic gospels)

The sending of the twelve: Matthew 9:37-10:42 (all of Luke 9:1-6; 10-11) (all of Luke 9 relevant to discipleship)

Sending of the Seventy: Luke 10:1-20

The call of Zacchaeus: Luke 19:1-10

The Risen Christ commissions Mary Magdalene: John 20:17-18

The Great Commission: Matthew 28:16; Luke 24:36-53

The conversion of Paul: Acts 9:1-9, and Ananias Acts 10-19

The call of Philip, and the conversion of Ethiopian: Acts 8:26-40

Notes

1. Sharon Daloz Parks, *Big Questions, Worthy Dreams: Mentoring Young Adults in their Search for Meaning, Purpose and Faith* (Jossey-Bass, 2000), 14.
2. Parks, 154–5.
3. Parks, 91.
4. Frederick Buechner, *Wishful Thinking: A Seeker's ABC* (New York: HarperOne, 1993), 118–119.
5. Kathleen Cahalan, *The Stories We Live* (Grand Rapids: Eerdmans, 2017).
6. Christopher Moore, *Lamb: The Gospel According to Biff, Christ's Childhood Pal* (New York: Harper, 2002), 340–342.
7. Richard Rohr, *Falling Upward: A Spirituality for the Two Halves of Life* (San Francisco: Jossey-Bass, 2011).
8. Kathleen Henderson Staudt, ed., *This Thing Called Poetry: An Anthology of Poetry by Young Adults with Cancer* (Georgetown KY: Finishing Line Press, 2019). Resources for people age 15–39 who have received a cancer diagnosis can be found at https://www.cancer.gov/types/aya/support.
9. Kathleen Henderson Staudt, "What I Remember," in *Waving Back: Poems of Mothering Life* (Georgetown KY: Finishing Line Press, 2009).
10. Evelyn Underhill, *The Spiritual Life* (1937; Harrisburg: Morehouse, 1955), 32.
11. For good guides to centering prayer, see Thomas Keating, *Intimacy with God: An Introduction to Centering Prayer* (New York: Crossroad, 2009) and Cynthia Bourgeault, *The Heart of Centering Prayer: Nondual Christianity in Theory and Practice* (Boulder: Shambala, 2016).
12. John Main, *Word into Silence: A Manual for Christian Meditation* (Norwich: Canterbury Press, 2006).
13. Brian McLaren, "Found in Translation," *Sojourners Magazine* (March 2006), http://sojo.net/index.cfm?action=magazine.article&issue=soj0603&article=060310.
14. Verna Dozier, *The Dream of God: A Call to Return* (1991; New York: Church Publishing, 2006).
15. Brian McLaren, *A Generous Orthodoxy* (Grand Rapids: Zondervan, 2004), 111.

16. Evelyn Underhill, *The School of Charity: Meditations on the Christian Creed* (1934; rpt. Harrisburg: Morehouse, 1994), 14–15.
17. For more on Ignatian spirituality, explore this website: http://ignatianspir ituality.com. Among the many good books in this tradition, I recommend James Martin, *The Jesuit Guide to Just About Everything* (New York: HarperOne, 2010).
18. For more on this memory, see Staudt, "Remembering the Company," in *Heaven*, ed. Roger Ferlo (New York: Seabury 2007), 187–195.
19. On the community that this gospel is addressed to, see Raymond Brown, *The Community of the Beloved Disciple* (Mahwah NJ: Paulist Press).
20. See Desmond Tutu, *God Has a Dream: A Vision of Hope for Our Time* (New York: Image Books, 2005), 20–21.
21. See http://www.couragerenewal.org/clearnesscommittee/. See also Parker Palmer, *A Hidden Wholeness: The Journey Toward an Undivided Life* (Hoboken: Jossey-Bass, 2004), 71–87 and *Let Your Life Speak: Listening to the Voice of Vocation* (Hoboken: Jossey-Bass, 1999).
22. Website for Nathan Dungan: http://www.sharesavespend.com.
23. Bonnie Thurston, *A Spirituality of Time* (Eugene, OR: Wipf and Stock, 2009)
24. The shape of this prayer is adapted from John Coburn's classic, *Prayer and Personal Religion*, revised and updated by Richard H. Schmidt (New York, Church Publishing, 2009).
25. Kathleen Cahalan, *The Stories We Live* (Grand Rapids MI: Eerdmans, 2017), 1–11.
26. William Stafford, "The Way It Is," in *Ask Me: 100 Essential Poems* (Minneapolis: Graywolf Press, 2004).
27. *The Way of a Pilgrim: Candid Tales of a Wanderer to his Spiritual Father*, ed. Andrew Louth and Anna Zaranko. (New York: Penguin Classics, 2019).
28. Denise Levertov, "Annunciation," in *The Door in the Hive* (New York: New Directions, 1989).
29. Richard Foster, *A Celebration of Discipline*. Third Edition (New York: HarperOne, 2009).
30. W. H. Auden, "For the Time Being," in *Collected Poems*, ed. Edward Mendelsohn (New York: Vintage Books, 1991), 400.
31. Esther de Waal, *Seeking God: The Way of St. Benedict* (Collegeville: Liturgical Press, 1984) pp. 41–84.
32. Esther de Waal, *Lost in Wonder: Rediscovering the Spiritual Art of Attentiveness* (Collegeville: Liturgical Press, 2003).
33. Brian McLaren, *A Generous Orthodoxy* (Grand Rapids, MI: Zondervan, 2004), 106–107.
34. This is the core argument of Howard Thurman's *Jesus and the Disinherited* (1949; Boston: Beacon Press, 1996).
35. Michael Curry, *Crazy Christians: A Call to Follow Jesus* (Harrisburg: Morehouse, 2013).

Further Reading on Discernment

Bankson, Marjory. *The Call to the Soul*. Augsburg, 2004.
A classic on the theme of "call"—details the "cycle of call" that we all experience.

De Waal, Esther. *Seeking God: The Way of St. Benedict*. 2nd ed., Liturgical Press, 2001.
———. *Lost in Wonder: Rediscovering the Spiritual Art of Attentiveness*. Liturgical Press, 2003.
Lived experience of Benedictine spirituality by a historian and spiritually grounded laywoman.

Cahalan, Kathleen A. *The Stories We Live: Finding God's Calling All around Us*. Eerdmans, 2017.
Some very useful exercises for reflecting on the experience of call in our lives, including in places we might not have thought to look.

Dozier, Verna. *The Dream of God: The Call to Return*. Seabury, 2021.
———. *Confronted by God: The Essential Verna Dozier*. Edited by Frederica Harris Thompsett and Cynthia L. Shattuck. Seabury, 2006.
A classic invitation to see our human stories within the story of salvation history by one of the twentieth century's most prophetic voices for the laity; contains tools for discerning God's purposes in our own time.

Johnson, Ben Campbell. *Hearing God's Call: Ways of Discernment for Clergy and Laity*. Eerdmans 2002.
In the reformed tradition: methodical approaches to listening for call.

Liebert, Elizabeth. *The Way of Discernment: Spiritual Practices for Decision Making*. Westminster John Knox, 2008.
Practical exercises based in the Ignatian tradition.

Nouwen, Henri. *Discernment: Reading the Signs of Daily Life*. HarperOne Reprint, 2013.
Personal story and spiritual wisdom offer tools for exploring our calling in the day to day experiences and relationships of our lives.

Palmer, Parker. *Let Your Life Speak: Listening to the Voice of Vocation*. Jossey-Bass, 2000.
———. *A Hidden Wholeness: The Journey toward an Undivided Life*. Jossey-Bass, 2009.
Along with thoughtful invitations to listening, both books offer insights into the value of the Quaker "clearness committee."

Underhill, Evelyn. *The Spiritual Life*. Church Publishing, 1993 (1936).
———. *Ways of the Spirit*. Edited by Grace Adolphsen Brame. Crossroad, 1993.
Among many writings of this important spiritual teacher.

Wolff, Pierre. *Discernment: The Art of Choosing Well*. Revised ed. Liguori, 2003.
One of the most accessible books I've found on discernment in the Ignatian tradition.